Medieval Knights

A Captivating Guide to the Knights of the Holy Sepulchre, Knights Hospitaller, Order of Saint Lazarus, Knights Templar, and Teutonic Knights

Free Bonus from Captivating History (Available for a Limited time)

Hi History Lovers!

Now you have a chance to join our exclusive history list so you can get your first history ebook for free as well as discounts and a potential to get more history books for free! Simply visit the link below to join.

Captivatinghistory.com/ebook

Also, make sure to follow us on Facebook, Twitter and Youtube by searching for Captivating History.

Table of Contents

Introduction

The mention of medieval knights often evokes images of massive horses pounding over vast plains and sand-strewn deserts, horses and men alike swathed in armor, with battle flags flying high. Or some might envision a Grail Knight guarding the Holy Chalice, like in the Indiana Jones movie where the knight cautions Indy to "choose wisely." Or even further back to Robert Taylor's rendition of Sir Lancelot in *Knights of the Round Table*, filmed in 1954. Through the ages, the imagery of brave knights found in books and movies is romantic and chivalric yet not always realistic.

Knights were known to surge into distant and foreign lands with firm beliefs and dedication to their religion. Many fought in the Holy Land against the "scourge of the Muslim hordes," while others fought against Germanic invaders or the pagans of eastern Europe.

They were formidable warriors, some with families, some living monkish lives. They fought bravely and lived violent, bloody lives. The medieval knights and their secret and not-so-secret orders and societies no doubt played a huge role in history, but even so, some are still shrouded in mystery.

A few are well known, at least by name. Some knightly orders or societies were dedicated to protecting pilgrims and saving lives, yet they became known as the most ferocious fighters of all. They fought for the preservation of Christianity and set out on crusades into the Holy Land, where religious wars were fought. Many of their legends have been passed down from generation to generation, while the origins and exploits of others are still shrouded in mystery.

Yet the life of the medieval knight encompassed many aspects of society and beliefs of their time. These men fought when called upon to do so, but just as often, they lived relatively ordinary lives at home. Some came from lowly origins, while others were descended from nobility or belonged to wealthy and aristocratic families.

They spent years as pages and squires and then, if they were fortunate and considered brave enough, became knights. Many pursued knighthoods for the excitement of battles, much like today's modern warriors. But they would soon realize that war was a bloody and dangerous business. They might have envisioned themselves riding mighty steeds in full armor, but in truth, thousands of knights marched toward their destinies on foot. Many fought without the benefit of armored suits.

Knights surged forth with an often single-minded purpose or desire to fight those they believed to be heretics and pagans, but there were just as many who fought for a sense of justice and religious fervor. Others fought for simpler things, such as rewards of money, land, booty, or, sometimes even more importantly, their reputation and pride.

The medieval ages spanned a period of time lasting approximately nine hundred years, and while the knights within many of the Christian orders fought for a certain cause, they also served different masters and kings.

Who were these knights? What was expected of them, and why did they spend so many years of their lives journeying to distant lands, often never to return? What happened to these orders through the medieval ages? And who led the knights into battle?

In this book, we'll explore some of these knightly orders, from the Hospitallers to the Teutonic Knights to Knights Templar. These knights made history. Their reputation and exploits have been handed down for centuries, so there is much for us to discover. Join us on a journey of these knightly brotherhoods and how they lived and fought and bled for what they believed in a time of uncertainty, war, and domination.

Chapter 1 – A Glimpse into the Middle Ages

Looking back through history, back through the centuries before the birth of Christianity, it seems as if mankind has always been fighting. They fought for land, sustenance, and their religions. Western Europe seemed to be constantly embroiled in war, and that did not change after the birth of Christianity.

The years from the 9th century (the 800s CE) through the 13th century (1200s CE) and beyond brought multiple and often violent clashes of nations, primarily between the Christians from western European countries and the populations to the east: the Magyars or Hungarian pagans, the Germanic hordes, and the Muslims from the deserts of the Middle East. Even western Europeans fought against one another, such as the English and the French; the squabbling often lasted generations.

Battles were waged near and far. Over time and over the multitudes of feudal wars that lasted for hundreds of years, castles were built, cavalries were formed, and warriors fought and died on hotly contested battlegrounds. Many of those mounted warriors who fought for one order or manor lord over another would today be called cavalry troops, but back in the day, they were known simply as mounted warriors before they became known as knights.

What made knights so special? They were often well trained, owned their own horses, and, if wealthy enough, were heavily armed and armored. Yet they were also known to be men who made vows of obedience, poverty, and chastity. It was a violent and bloody time to live, yet these knights were sworn to bravery, to serve others and a higher power, and to live by certain rules that are now known as the code of chivalry. History tells us they were polite, courteous, and sometimes even generous. Yet most of all, they personified the ideas of valor, gallantry, and bravery against all odds, ideas that have been passed down through the centuries that followed.

These warriors were honor-bound and loyal to the feudal system to which they belonged, but they fought not only for what they believed in but also in the hopes of providing honorable and loyal service that might enable them to earn a reward of land or a manor of their own.

Some of these men returned home to great acclaim, including Alfred the Great and Charlemagne. Eventually, the status of these mounted warriors, who later became known as knights, received special notice and honor. They belonged to what was otherwise known as a brotherhood—a brotherhood of knights serving one master or another. Their kings. Their religion. Their sense of justice.

For many centuries, noble and lowborn fought side by side, yet it was mostly the nobles or the wealthy who were found in these groups since they were able to afford the cost of fighting equipment and horses.

For a time, these knightly groups or orders were composed of those with elite status, such as members of wealthy households, landowners, or varying ranks of nobility. Eventually, that changed, especially in England. Nevertheless, these groups of men created a fraternity of sorts, representing valor, courage, honor, and duty. They were blessed by the church as defenders of the Christian faith. They believed that the battles they fought were not merely holy but also sacred, following the brave examples of the biblical David, Joshua, and Gideon who came before them.

Within three centuries after the death of Christ, the justification for such battles and wars was that they were noble and right. They believed in the words of Aristotle, the Greek philosopher, and the leaders of ancient Rome, who said that any war that attempted to recover a seized piece of property or territory or that defended one's beliefs was fought on God's authority. Knights became generally known as defenders of the faith and Christian warriors engaged in a holy war.

Christian fervor was found on many battlefields throughout the centuries, and artifacts from the time display Christian images on weapons, further justifying their fight to overcome paganism and vindicating their efforts to convert their enemies to Christianity and spread the faith. It was an era that sought greater protection for the church and the protection of the weak, meaning clergy, monks, and pilgrims. The knights wanted to promote the idea of justice not only in their native lands but also in foreign lands as well.

It was also a time of inner conflict for many of these knightly warriors in regard to their Christian faith. History tells us that even the soldiers who fought under William the Conqueror in the Battle of Hastings were required to perform penance for the blood spilled on the battlefield, even though they had fought valiantly under the papal banner.

The medieval ages, also known as the Middle Ages or the Dark Ages, encompassed the time between the fall of the Roman Empire and the Renaissance: in other words, from around 476 to the 16th century CE. This period is typically identified by three primary timeframes, known as the Early Middle Ages, the High Middle Ages, and the Late Middle Ages.

In essence, these centuries were consumed by bloody battles and religious fervor, with few developments or advancements in technology, literature, or art, hence the nickname the "Dark Ages." This era saw the bubonic plague, more commonly known as the Black Death, which started around 1346 and ended in 1353, although outbreaks continued to happen over the years. Nearly twenty-five million people died throughout Europe.

However, the medieval era was also a time that promoted the spread of Christianity from its origins in the Holy Land (the lands of Israel and Palestine). In eras past, these lands were known as the land of the Hittites. The term Asia Minor was coined to avoid confusion with the regions visited by the Apostle Paul.

Over a millennium before the fall of Rome, Alexander the Great conquered much of Asia Minor, but the region continued to be a land troubled by instability. After the fall of Rome around 476 CE, the region became known as the Byzantine Empire (although, at the time, the people living there considered themselves to be part of the Roman Empire).

Within a century after the decline of the Roman Empire, another religion swept through what is known today as the Middle East. This religion was Islam. Its followers, like the Christian knights who followed their faith, believed in the teachings of the Prophet Muhammad. Each group saw the other as infidels. What followed were centuries of fighting. It was a time of great upheaval in the Byzantine Empire, as the Muslims rose up and conquered lands, encompassing a huge area that on maps today incorporates the lands of Pakistan on their eastern border to the Moroccan region to the south and the current regions of Spain and Portugal, known as the Iberian Peninsula, to the west. During these years, Christianity also spread. The fighting continued, and the occupation of the Holy Land was hotly contested.

By the end of the 1st millennium, the German Empire was also in turmoil, with localized groups all vying for control. The Habsburg dynasty provided a vague sense of unity at the time, though princes throughout the land still fought one another for power. Yet, despite the infighting, Germany was a force to be reckoned with and used its growing power to influence countries around them to embrace Christianity. At the time, Germany had a huge influence that some historians have compared to that of ancient Rome.

During those years, thousands of Christians began to make pilgrimages to the Holy Land. They were sponsored by the church to visit and worship at holy sites and shrines throughout the region.

The Pilgrimages

Pilgrimages to the Holy Land turned, for all intents and purposes, into a tradition, a way for people to achieve a cleansing of their sins and souls. These pilgrims came from many different lands and made the journey to the holiest city of all—Jerusalem—in an effort to gain atonement for their sins and gain penance through the harsh sacrifices they endured during their journey. Most of these individuals came from higher classes of society because, quite frankly, they could afford it.

They came by the dozens and then by the hundreds and then often by the thousands. Men, women, children, and servants traveled through harsh and dangerous landscapes to prove to their priests and to their Lord that they were sorry for their sins and offenses to God and man alike. The journey to the Holy Land was only part of their penance, as they were also required to give money or aid to those less fortunate than themselves. Before they could even make the journey, they had to receive permission from their priest; otherwise, their pilgrimage wouldn't count, spiritually at least. After their return, the priest would pardon their sins.

By the dawn of the 2nd century, Jerusalem had become the primary destination for such pilgrimages, and by the 4th century (the 1300s), historical writings describe sizable Christian pilgrimages to the city of Jerusalem. Once in the Holy City, these pilgrims sought out famous sites mentioned in the Bible.

Constantine the Great (Roman emperor from 306 to 337 CE) is believed to have directed the building of churches and identified sacred sites, such as the reputed place of Christ's burial. There, Constantine directed the construction of the Church of the Holy Sepulchre in 325 CE.

However, during the height of the pilgrimages, the practice of Islam also began to spread, especially during the centuries following the death of their prophet, Muhammad, the founder of the Islam faith, in 632. They, like the Christians, believed they were fighting for what was right and sought to gain control of the Holy Land, which was also a sacred site to their faith.

Even before the years of the First Crusade in 1096, the expansion of Islam encompassed great swathes of territory, eventually spreading from the depths of the Middle East westward along the southern banks of the Mediterranean Sea to the west and north and east into the former Persian Empire, bordering the Caspian and Arabian Seas, and to the Byzantine Empire, nestled between the northern shores of the Mediterranean Sea to the Black Sea.

Land boundaries changed over the years, making the medieval era a time of conquests and migrations. Those of Slavic and Germanic nationalities migrated throughout Europe. The Goths played a large role in the Western Roman Empire's destruction and were also influential in the early years of the Middle Ages. The Goths were known as barbarians; they were seen as violent, uneducated, and unsophisticated. During the 4th century, the Visigoth leader, Athanaric, didn't much care for the "new Roman religion," otherwise known as Christianity, fearing that the religion would influence the Goths and make them abandon tradition.

During the Middle Ages, massive numbers of pilgrims ventured over land and sea to reach the Holy Land. For generations, making a pilgrimage as a form of penance and overcoming its hardships became a common practice. And who better to protect those pilgrims but brave knights? The men who joined the brotherhoods of chivalric knights were, perhaps like many throughout history, lured by the excitement of foreign lands and battles. Many of them lived like monks, vowing obedience, austerity, and even chastity. It was a brotherhood in the truest sense of the word. They ate together, slept together, fought together, and often died together.

During these turbulent years, numerous knightly societies or orders were founded. Some are more well known than others, such as, for instance, the Templars and the Hospitallers. They spanned a timeframe that encompassed numerous crusades or religious wars between Christians and Muslims with the goal of controlling sacred and holy sites throughout the regions of what is known today as the Middle East.

These orders were formed to protect and wrest the Holy Land from the Muslims, who had gained control of it toward the end of the Byzantine Empire. The orders also wanted to spread the message of Christianity to the pagans of Europe. While the vast majority of men who joined these orders were former cavalry soldiers or warriors, most were already knights. Many of these orders were known as religious military societies or orders, including the Hospitallers (originally a group of monks seeking to protect pilgrims journeying to the Holy Land), the Knights Templar, and the Teutonic Knights, all of whom had the same goals in mind.

Who founded these knightly societies and orders? Who were these men who fought for God and Christianity, and what happened to them?

Chapter 2 – The Crusades: A Brief Overview

No history or glimpse into the lives of the medieval knights and their orders would be possible without providing a brief overview of the Crusades, which are primarily defined as religious wars that spanned centuries.

The major Crusades took place over a nearly two-hundred-year span of time. Different orders were prevalent during one or more of the Crusades, which resulted in thousands of lives lost, cities destroyed, and the nearly ongoing resentment from both sides.

These decades spanned empires and involved kings and emirs. Some of the major players came from the thrones of England, France, Germany, the Byzantine Empire, and the Islamic caliphates. These were years fraught with battles and skirmishes over land, the right to rule, and even infighting among groups from a varied number of countries.

The First Crusade: 1096–1099

Over time, Christians became divided between the Roman Catholics and the Eastern Orthodox Christians; this event was later known as the Great Schism of 1054. The divisions within the Catholic Church eventually provided the birth and growth of the Protestant Reformation, which, in turn, triggered several political and religious disagreements.

The First Crusade began at a time when a Byzantine general-turned-emperor by the name of Alexius Comnenus requested aid from Pope Urban II to help prevent the Turks from encroaching on the eastern Byzantine provinces. What he really wanted was soldiers. The request came at an opportune time, as the pope at that time had been urging Christians throughout the west to support the Byzantines in their efforts to push back the Muslims, who had taken over many holy sites throughout the Middle East. The pope's goal was to recapture and control the Holy Land.

At that time, thousands of soldiers answered the call. Some went on foot or on horseback. Some of these armies were organized and led by experienced knights or those with military knowledge, while others were less organized, with some being led by clergymen or those seeking the glory of participating in a holy war. The politics of the regions and the allegiance of armies at the time were relatively fluid, and Alexius demanded that the armies arriving in his lands swear loyalty to him. He also insisted that he maintain control over any land won by the crusading armies. However, most of these knights declined to do so.

They fought together anyway, and by 1097, the Byzantines and their allies attacked Nicaea, which is today found in Turkey. The battle was important, as it was one of the first great battles that set the stage for the Crusades.

The Siege of Nicaea

The siege of Nicaea was where the soldiers of the Crusades first made a name for themselves. The city of Nicaea is an ancient Christian site; the first council of the Christian Church gathered there in 325. During this council, the Christian doctrine known as the Nicene Creed was agreed upon. For centuries, the city of Nicaea, which was less than one hundred miles from the city of Constantinople, had been part of the Byzantine Empire. The city fell to the Seljuk Turks in 1081.

At the time of the First Crusade, Nicaea was the capital of the Seljuk Turks, and as long as the capital remained in Turkish hands, the advance toward Jerusalem could not be achieved.

However, to think of the soldiers involved in the First Crusade as an organized, disciplined, and orderly army would be incorrect. They were highly disorganized, owing to the vast number of men involved, and their numbers were rife with rivalries, language and cultural barriers, and disciplinary issues, primarily because there was fighting and arguing among the lords and commanders who oversaw them.

Added to the cacophony were the civilians who accompanied the soldiers, non-combatants that included women and children. Some of the civilians were family members of the soldiers, while others were making pilgrimages or belonged to the clergy. Also joining the crusaders was a large force of Byzantine soldiers, approximately two thousand under the command of Tatikios, who had made a name for himself defending Constantinople against European peasants in 1096.

Yes, many were eager to make their devotion to God known, including the poor. The Peasants' Crusade (a rather unsuccessful effort by untrained peasants to help push back and defeat the encroaching Turks) saw tens of thousands of peasants make their way to the Holy Land; almost all of them died since they were not experienced in warfare or lacked the proper equipment.

The crusaders didn't arrive as one unified force at Nicaea. Among the first were knights under Godfrey of Bouillon and Robert of Flanders, a son of William the Conqueror. The final contingent of forces arrived under Robert of Normandy and Stephen of Blois by early June.

The crusaders managed to surround three sides of the city and settled in for an extended siege due to the fact they were unable to block the lake approach to the city (Lake Ascania), through which the enemy ensconced in Nicaea could receive supplies.

Early in the siege, the sultan of the Turkish state called Rum returned to the city from abroad, as he had been fighting another rival. He was apparently startled by the massive forces that had gathered at the capital. He quickly launched a surprise attack on one of the armies of Raymond of Toulouse, which turned out to be successful for the crusaders, especially after Godfrey of Bouillon sent reinforcements.

The siege of Nicaea lasted six long weeks, but the siege equipment was not capable of causing any real damage to the city walls. According to historical documents, a number of objects were catapulted over the walls, including beehives, rocks, detached heads of corpses, and flaming missiles. The more common goal of a siege is to starve the enemy out, but that would not happen due to the sultan's access to the lake.

Meanwhile, Emperor Alexius hoped that Nicaea would not be destroyed since his goal was to add it to the Byzantine Empire. So, he initiated an end run, to use today's American football parlance, and made secret negotiations with the Turks, promising them safety if they surrendered.

Imagine the crusaders' surprise when, in mid-June, upon their preparation to initiate a major attack on Nicaea, the crusaders spied the Byzantine standard flying high above the walls. The Byzantine troops had already gained control of the city. The crusader leaders were likely quite frustrated, especially since the Byzantine troops only allowed small groups of crusaders into the city, making their "apologies" to the crusader commanders with gifts of jewelry, wine, and foodstuffs. Naturally, the knights were more than a little unhappy, as they had been planning to score some loot from the city.

In spite of infighting and increasing resentment between the Byzantine soldiers and their leaders and those of the crusaders, the united force went on to capture Antioch, a Syrian city, in 1098 and then headed for Jerusalem, which at the time was occupied by the Seljuks. The conflicts of this region felt as if they were never-ending (they actually continue to this day), but by 1099, the Christian crusaders forced the surrender of the Muslims occupying the city of Jerusalem. After this, the crusaders founded the Kingdom of Jerusalem, which would last for nearly two centuries.

After Jerusalem was captured, most of the knights and soldiers returned to their homes, leaving behind four primary settlements in the conquered region that were formed into what is known as the Crusader States or Outremer. These states remained under the tenuous control of the Christian crusaders from about 1098 to 1291. These states came to include Jerusalem to the south, Tripoli to the north, Antioch even farther north, and then Edessa, which was even farther north between the Euphrates and Tigris Rivers.

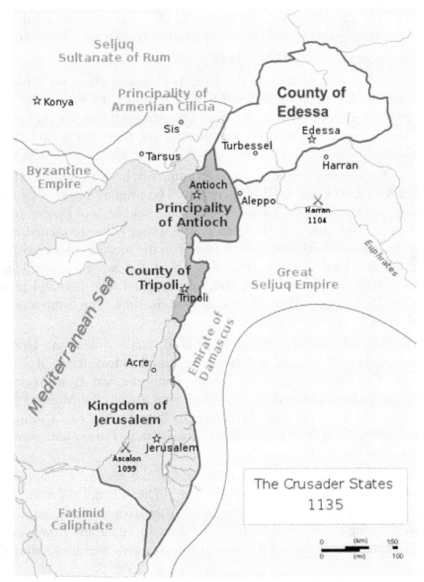

A map of the Crusader States in 1135.
Amitchell125, CC BY-SA 4.0 <https://creativecommons.org/licenses/by-sa/4.0>, via Wikimedia Commons; https://commons.wikimedia.org/wiki/File:The_Crusader_States_in_1135.svg

The First Crusade was over, and for nearly fifty years, an uneasy détente of sorts existed. Councils were constructed, and the area maintained a relatively peaceful existence until Muslim forces began a new jihad or holy war against the Christians in about 1130 CE.

In 1144, a Seljuk general by the name of Zengi recaptured Edessa, the northernmost state, and rumors of another crusade began to spread.

The Second Crusade: 1147-1149

The orders of knights, like the Knights Hospitaller and the Knights Templar, took part in the Second Crusade. Some orders, such as the Hospitallers, existed prior to the First Crusade but provided aid to the sick and gave care to traveling pilgrims making their way to the Holy Land.

The Second Crusade was overseen primarily by King Louis VII of France and King Conrad III of Germany. The primary objective of this crusade was to recapture Edessa. Once again, soldiers and knights rode off to war. Unfortunately, King Conrad's forces were decimated at a place known as Dorylaeum, which had been the location of a Christian victory in the First Crusade. After that defeat, the two European kings joined forces in Jerusalem and, with an estimated fifty thousand men, attacked Damascus, a Muslim stronghold at the time. The battle was yet another failure for the crusaders.

The Second Crusade, though short-lived, was a violent and bloody affair, yet when all was said and done, the crusaders had managed to win a number of battles within the Iberian Peninsula and Baltic regions. They successfully defeated the Muslims, even though the Muslims had called for aid from the ruler of Damascus (Syria) and Zengi's son and eventual successor, Nur al-Din, from Mosul (Iraq). Edessa remained in the hands of Nur al-Din.

However, in the years between the end of the Second Crusade and the beginning of the Third Crusade, Nur al-Din was not dormant. He eventually became the emir of Damascus. After having made a name for himself during the Second Crusade, he grew in might and power, and by 1154, he had absorbed Damascus into his own rapidly expanding empire.

The Third Crusade: 1189-1192

Nearly forty years passed between the end of the Second Crusade and the beginning of the Third Crusade. In brief, the Third Crusade was launched to regain control of the lands along the eastern shores and lands bordering the eastern Mediterranean region—the lands primarily claimed as Crusader States following the end of the First Crusade—and to protect their hold on Jerusalem

Conflicts continued to roil among the former forces of Nur al-Din, who had died in 1174. Saladin, who came from a family that had served Nur al-Din, made a name for himself on several military forays. Due to his prowess and despite his young age (he was just over thirty years old), he became the sultan of Syria and Egypt shortly after Nur al-Din's death.

While Nur al-Din had failed to gain control of Jerusalem in his lifetime, Saladin set his sights on capturing the city. By 1187, Saladin had gone on the offensive, wanting to drive the Christian crusaders from the Kingdom of Jerusalem once and for all. He nearly destroyed the crusaders at the Battle of Hattin (present-day Israel).

The Battle of Hattin and the loss of so many Christian soldiers led to the outbreak of the Third Crusade, which was led by King Richard I (Richard the Lionheart), Holy Roman Emperor Frederick Barbarossa, and King Philip II of France.

The German Crusader

Frederick I, better known as Frederick Barbarossa, which in Italian means "Red Beard," reigned as the Holy Roman emperor from 1152 to 1190. He partook in two crusades (the second and the third) but died during the Third Crusade. He drowned while crossing a river in what is now Turkey on his way to the Holy Land.

Frederick I gained a reputation as a great German ruler, and like others of his time, legends surround him. Some legends say he did not die and that he is simply sleeping in a cave in the mountains of central Germany to come forth when his native land needs him the most.

An image of Frederick Barbarossa, "Red Beard."

https://www.ancient-origins.net/history/frederick-i-barbarossa-megalomaniac-roman-emperor-crusade-power-008283

According to historical writings and legends, Frederick I was determined to restore the empire that had been established by Charlemagne. He managed to negotiate and encourage peace between numerous princes within his lands. He also took part in many campaigns, half a dozen of which were in Italy, in an effort to emphasize his imperial rights. During Barbarossa's first visit there in 1155, he ensured his coronation as Holy Roman emperor by Pope Adrian IV but was ultimately excommunicated in 1160 after legalities involving one of the church's lawyers and a hopeful pope, Alexander III, who desired to ensure a papacy that was independent of the Holy Roman Empire.

Over the following years, Frederick refused to recognize Alexander III as pope, and in 1167, during his fourth journey to Italy, where he intended to best Alexander, he was forced to give up on his goals since a plague (some sources say malaria) broke out. It wasn't until 1177 that Frederick recognized Alexander III as the pope.

When the Third Crusade broke out in 1189, Frederick I had taken up the cross and gathered a large army of Germans that is said to have been three thousand strong. They set out for the Holy Land and reached Constantinople in 1189. As Barbarossa captured one city after another, Muslims in the region grew increasingly concerned, especially Saladin, who gathered his own army to confront him.

Unfortunately for the crusaders, in early June 1190, Frederick fell from his horse while crossing the Saleph River and drowned. The exact cause of his death is unknown, but some believe that his armor weighed him down or that he experienced a heart attack caused by the shockingly cold water. Either way, he drowned, even though historical accounts state that the water was only waist-high.

At any rate, the Third Crusade was effectively over as far as his men were concerned. Many returned home, though others continued under the command of his son, Frederick of Swabia, who led them to join other crusaders at the siege of Acre on the northern borders of present-day Israel.

Some accounts relate that Barbarossa's son transported his body the entire way, hoping to bury him in Jerusalem. Apparently, Frederick of Swabia tried to preserve the body through the use of vinegar. Legend also has it that Barbarossa's decaying flesh was boiled from his bones and that the remnants of his army carried his bones all the way to Tyre, where he was ultimately buried.

Meanwhile, in the autumn of 1191, King Richard I's army defeated Saladin during the Battle of Arsuf, which, curiously enough, would be about the only large-scale battle that occurred during the Third Crusade. Most of the remainder of this crusade was relegated to skirmishes and clashes until Saladin signed a peace treaty with King Richard about a year later, in 1192. The peace treaty reestablished the Kingdom of Jerusalem under Christian rule but, oddly enough, did not include the actual city of Jerusalem. However, although the city would remain under Islamic control, Christian pilgrims were welcome to journey there.

The Fourth Crusade: 1202–1204

Peace in the region didn't last for long, as powers throughout western Europe to the Middle East and farther eastward played a tug-of-war for supremacy, though many of the issues that triggered conflicts existed between the European kingdoms and the Byzantine Empire. At the time, Pope Innocent III encouraged another crusade, but this time, it wasn't merely over religion but also the time-old concept of power and control over lands. And, of course, wresting Jerusalem from the grasp of the Muslims was at the top of the list.

The new crusade was answered, with many French barons being among the crusaders. They contracted with the Venetians for provisions and ships to take them to the Holy Land. The Venetians had their own grudges against the Byzantine Empire but agreed to supply the pope's army with a fleet of ships and enough provisions to last nine months. The crusaders faced a high cost and were further burdened by the Venetians' demand to receive roughly one-half of the plunder seized by the crusaders. Not all of the crusaders were able to make the journey, so when the crusaders made it to Venice, they realized they could not pay the Venetians what they owed.

The Venetians decided the crusaders could pay them back in a different way. They could attack ports along the coast, with Zara (located in modern-day Croatia) being the main prize. Even though Zara was a primarily Christian city, the Venetians wanted to gain it back, having lost it about twenty years prior. The pope learned about it and threatened the crusaders with excommunication if they attacked a Christian city, but they felt forced to proceed since they were obligated to pay off their debts.

Unfortunately, the sacking of Zara failed to provide enough loot to repay the Venetians. Constantinople was facing some difficulties, and the Venetians saw its trouble as a chance to gain funds. The crusaders initially arrived in Constantinople to help deal with the succession crisis. The aspiring emperor had promised them riches, but when he became emperor, he realized the treasury was dangerously low. He was unable to pay the crusaders what he promised. Tensions built up until the crusaders essentially rioted, destroying the city. The crusaders descended into lawlessness and abhorrent behavior and slaughtered many of the city's inhabitants.

The Significance of Constantinople

The significance of Constantinople (located in present-day Turkey) should not be underestimated. The city was located on a spit of land that connected Europe to the west with the landmass of Asia Minor to the east. The Black Sea was to the north, and the Aegean Sea just to the south, with the Mediterranean beyond that.

Since its founding in the 4th century by Constantine, the city of Constantinople was perceived as a symbolic rebirth of Rome. It became the center of clashes between the East and West and between Muslims and Christians. Following the Great Schism of 1054, the city became the most important city of the Eastern Orthodox Church. The Great Schism saw the splintering of the Christian Church into two factions: the Roman Catholic Church and the Eastern Orthodox Church.

Constantinople was engaged in a near-constant tug-of-war between various factions that included the Arabs, Bulgarians, and other European Christians. But in 1204, the crusaders plundered the city, drove the Byzantines out, and created a Latin state. In 1261, the Byzantines again took control of the city, and though it was no longer nearly as grand as it once had been, it was still a highly populated port city.

Eventually, the city again became the center of a tug-of-war for power, and in 1453, it was overtaken by Mehmed II for the Ottoman Empire. Once more, the city found itself under Muslim rule.

The fall of Constantinople in late May 1453 occurred after a fifty-five-day siege. Mehmed's success was primarily due to his use of gunpowder and cannons, which decimated the once-powerful city and its defenses.

The actual fall of Constantinople gives us a fascinating glimpse into the tenacity of an outnumbered force that fought valiantly to defend the great city, one that was subdued by the ongoing onslaught on its walls by Mehmed's artillery barrage.

During the following decades, the formerly Christian churches in the city were converted into mosques, except for the Church of Saint Mary of the Mongols. Perhaps surprisingly, Mehmed II tolerated a diverse religious population and is known to have encouraged those from different faiths and backgrounds to populate the city. From 1520 through 1566, the Ottoman Empire was ruled by Suleyman the Magnificent, who expanded the Ottoman Empire. Today, scholars often mark the fall of Constantinople as the end of the medieval or Middle Ages and the dawn of the Renaissance.

The Fifth Crusade (1217–1271)

Following the sacking of Constantinople during the Fourth Crusade, a number of crusaders marched into the Middle East and the Holy Land, with their goal now primarily being to engage in skirmishes and fights against any and all who were seen as "enemies of the Christian faith." Of course, Muslim forces felt the same way about the Christians, so it was a time of open conflicts that accomplished nothing much except bloodshed and the loss of men on both sides.

A proper crusade had to be sanctioned by the church, though. The Fifth Crusade again focused on recapturing Jerusalem, and in 1215, Pope Innocent III began to call upon knights and other able-bodied men to help achieve this by weakening the bonds that the Egyptian Ayyubid state had on the city and its surrounding lands. This time, though, the crusade was to be guided more directly by the church to avoid another major incident of crusaders going rogue, as had happened during the Fourth Crusade. However, by this time, many knights and soldiers were weary of near-constant warring, and interest was lukewarm at best.

The pope then called on the general populace and effectively "encouraged" them to join the crusade, promising them monetary rewards. Before that could be accomplished, Pope Innocent passed away, with his place being taken by Pope Honorius III, who then took over the organization of the crusade.

However, after gathering at Acre, the new group of crusaders, along with a number of French knights that bolstered their numbers, headed for Egypt. Their first goal was to take a city named Damietta, and then they would continue to Cairo. By the time they reached that city, they believed the Egyptian hold on the lands should be significantly weakened.

While the crusaders managed to drive the Egyptians from Damietta, their lack of knowledge of the area proved to be their downfall. They failed to take into account the season, and the Nile flooded. When they finally decided to turn back, they were attacked by the Egyptians, causing the loss of many crusaders.

Although there were other crusades, the Fifth Crusade was one of the last that really captivated the people enough to join. During the Sixth Crusade (1228–1229), Jerusalem would be regained. The last official crusade, the Eighth Crusade (1270), saw no advances made in the Middle East. About twenty years later, Acre fell, leading to the end of the Crusader States.

Numerous forays were made to the Holy Land during the Crusades, with one of the most unusual made by a surprising contingent of European citizenry.

The Children's Crusade

In 1212, something extraordinary happened, and while it isn't exactly considered an official crusade and did not include the medieval knights, it did include thousands of pilgrims vowing to march to Jerusalem. What was different about this crusade was that it was composed of thousands of young children. Today, it is called the Children's Crusade. According to historical documents, tens of thousands of people set out on the journey, even though rulers and the pope told them to return home. It wasn't only children and teenagers who joined in but also women, the poor, and the elderly. Basically, the outliers of society, the ones who were often rendered "invisible" from the wealthy or well-to-do of their times, were part of this crusade.

The group was led by twelve-year-old shepherd Stephen of Cloyes. Young Stephen held some sway over his followers and is believed to embody a boldness that likely took many by surprise. He even demanded to see the king of France (and did) to receive permission to conduct the crusade. But what was his goal? He wanted to reclaim the Holy Land for the Catholic Church and remove Muslims from Jerusalem.

Twelve-year-old Stephen of Cloyes was a unique young boy who gained attention and claimed to have experienced a vision that was divine in nature. Despite the king's warning not to proceed, young Stephen gained quite a following, and being a stubborn young man, he proceeded with his dream of accomplishing something great for Christianity. The mass of children and adults headed out, but they were ill-equipped, ill-provisioned, and mostly unarmed.

Little is known of their actual pilgrimage, and some historians today question the crusade's veracity. Since the crusade was not condoned by the pope, it was never declared an actual crusade. Nevertheless, the majority of historians believe it occurred. The group of children and adults ventured forward, but instead of carrying weapons, they carried crosses and banners. The youth must have been convinced that they could accomplish things the adults never could. They were convinced and very optimistic that once they reached the Holy Land, they would be able to convert the Muslims into Christians through divine intervention.

And it wasn't Stephen of Cloyes alone who led this crusade. Another group was also whipped into a frenzy of religious fervor, this one led by a young man named Nicholas of Cologne.

At any rate, the crusaders gathered in Marseille to prepare for the crossing of the Mediterranean before heading farther into the Holy Land. According to legend, they waited for the miracle that Stephen insisted would happen but didn't: the Mediterranean would part as the Red Sea did for Moses as he led his people to freedom. Many of his followers returned home. While Stephen of Cloyes's group waited on the banks of the Mediterranean for passage, the young German from Cologne took his group toward the Alps, also heading for Jerusalem.

What was unique about the Children's Crusade was its ability to gain attention not only from children but also from families in towns throughout western Europe. While their religious beliefs were no doubt firm, they were able to motivate the crowds like the popes had been able to do in previous crusades. As such, they might have been viewed less enthusiastically by the church, whose priests might have been somewhat concerned that they would lose some of their respect and control over the populace.

The church called these crusaders fanatics, and yet their very presence created curiosity throughout the land. These two child leaders of two different groups gave their sermons and spoke of miracles. They likely left their listeners spellbound.

Ultimately, both groups failed in their mission. Nicholas of Cologne and his followers did make it far, although they quickly ran out of food and became exhausted. They pressed on and finally managed to make it to Genoa, Italy. There, they were unable to communicate with the locals, who, as history tells it, weren't too thrilled with the sudden arrival of hundreds of starving children. As can be imagined, some of them met tragic fates. Some starved, some were forced to take local jobs to fund their return home, and some were sold into slavery. Others managed to gain passage on ships, with some of them being drowned at sea.

While the actual size and events of the Children's Crusade are difficult to historically verify, it does show the religious fervor of the times.

The first five crusades encapsulated some of the harshest years of the Middle Ages, but during these challenging times, the knights of old made their mark on history forever. However, not just anyone could become a knight. To do so required a unique character and a willingness to sacrifice. For some, this journey took years.

Chapter 3 – The Journey to Knighthood

When one hears the words "medieval knights," the first thing that often comes to mind is men wearing armor, maybe with fancy plumes of feathers or perhaps a swath of horsehair trailing from atop their metal helmets. They sit on their mighty stallions, a long jousting pole tucked under one arm, the other tightly grasping his horse's reins as he charges toward an opponent at the tournament, determined to win the hand of a fair lady.

A number of myths about knights persist even today, such as those in full armor needing a crane-like contraption to be hoisted onto their mighty steeds. How awkward would it have been if they were knocked off their horse in battle?

Another myth is that knights were only those of noble birth. In the knighthood's earliest stages, more were from the aristocracy or nobility, but how could an order create an army of knights if only those with a certain pedigree were allowed? Men of lowly birth were often knighted following acts of valor or courage or for their loyalty to the knights they served. In some cases, their knighthood could be bought.

Not all knights donned full suits of armor; instead, some used bits and pieces of armor that were gathered as booty from a battlefield or won during a tournament. Armor, like anything manufactured today, was not always high-quality either. At any rate, it was more common for a knight to focus his need for armor on vulnerable body parts, such as the head, the hands, and the torso. Full suits of armor were constructed of metal strips that were attached with leather straps and movable links that allowed amazing freedom of joint movement. Heavy, yes, but they were not stiff and unwieldy.

The knight was supposed to personify chivalry and bravery, one who was duty- and honor-bound to defend not only the kingdom but also everyone in it. However, not every brave or chivalrous man had what it took to become a knight in the medieval ages. And as time passed, knights fell prey to corruption, seeking treasures instead of honor.

Perhaps most important of all, one who desired to become a knight was required to start at the bottom rung of the ladder, so to speak. They learned by doing. Typically, a future knight began his training as a young boy between seven and ten years of age. The boy would be charged with caring for a knight's horses. He was called a page, and he was an assistant of sorts to a knight. In the majority of cases, the page also came from an aristocratic family but not always. It was the page's duty to learn the ways of war, how to care for weapons, manners, and obedience.

During a page's daily activities, he might spend his time ensuring the cleanliness and readiness of the knight or nobleman's weaponry, caring for his horses, and even dressing the knight and aiding in the donning of his armor. After all, a complete suit of armor at the time weighed anywhere between thirty and fifty pounds (fourteen to twenty-three kilograms). Suits of armor were often cumbersome and difficult to don by oneself. The page was also responsible for ensuring that the leather straps and rivets that held the strips of metal together were kept in good condition.

Over time, the page was taught skills that would serve him well throughout life, such as hunting, horsemanship, and the wielding of weaponry commonly used by knights. Yet their days were not only filled with menial labor or learning how to fight. If the page was fortunate and had an educated knight as a mentor, he might also be taught a number of additional life skills, including reading and writing. He would also be taught what was expected in regard to behavior, courtesy, and manners in courtly environments. After all, the knight a page served might have to visit the royal court or receive orders from the lord of the manor, their feudal lord, or a fiefdom they served. In their spare time, pages might be taught subjects like music, art, and even poetry.

In return for their diligence and devotion, a page could expect to receive food, clothing, and shelter from the knight or nobleman they served. In some circumstances, and depending on the level of their service and dedication, a page might also receive a reward from the person they served, be it monetary or material.

After enough time passed, the page advanced to the next stage.

To Squire...

Typically, young boys could expect to serve a knight or nobleman as a page until they turned thirteen or fourteen, upon which they could be promoted to the position of squire. They would be required to spend about the same amount of time as a knight's squire.

Squires not only provided care for the knights they served but also for their lords of the realm, especially the lord that their knight served. Therefore, the squire not only assisted the knight when it came to tournaments or battle, but they also basically existed as servants in a manor house or castle if it were so desired by their lord.

Even after the conclusion of their seven years of serving as a squire, some of these young men continued to serve their knights or lords as squires well into adulthood. Some even served their entire lives because they never attained the rank of knighthood.

During tournaments, the squire was required to prepare the knight's horse and equipment, including his lance. A squire was supposed to always be ready to provide assistance. They learned how to handle common battle swords, as well as the heaviest two-handed swords, which could weigh as much as forty-five pounds (twenty kilograms), although most of the one- and two-handed swords often weighed anywhere between four pounds (two kilograms) and ten pounds (five kilograms).

In times of peace, they were taught what could be deemed daily activities, such as hunting, dancing, and some education in history. They enhanced their equestrian skills and learned how to joust. They were trained in numerous fighting styles, both with and without armor. Squires also served their knights during times of war and often accompanied them into battle.

By doing this, a squire was able to show he had the mettle to become a knight. This didn't happen overnight. The process could take years. If a squire proved his bravery and stoutness in battle and in service by having a good and obedient demeanor, he was often recommended for a knighthood. At this time, he would generally wear clothing and armor that identified him under the particular coat of arms of the knight he served. Some knights were able to earn great rewards, including lands and titles, depending on their performance and loyalty on the battlefield and their years of service.

One of the most important things taught to young knights was the concept of chivalry, which is basically a code of conduct. This was required of knights, squires, and pages. After being knighted, a knight promised loyalty to the feudal lord under whom he served. Of course, one of the most important traits a knight had to have was bravery. To not serve with bravery was to invite complete humiliation, not only by his peers but also by the general public as well.

The Idea of Chivalry as Epitomized by the Knights

The knights' code of conduct was not only related to bravery on the battlefield; it also emphasized service. Some codes of conduct stressed valor, bravery, generosity, and a willingness to serve others, not only through offering protection but also through their everyday actions and deeds. The code of conduct was not something that was recited from a piece of paper. It was a concept of behavior that was part of a young man's training as a page and squire.

The centuries of the medieval age encompassed a dark and bloody period of history. Yet, during those years, a knight was expected to be brave and gentle (primarily toward women and children). He was expected to offer protection for those who were defenseless or too weak to fight for themselves. They were sworn to protect their faith and their church, to live with honor, and to serve their feudal lords and kings without question.

Knights were also given codes of conduct by the feudal lords they served, which often included rules regarding positive characteristics, such as being prudent, truthful, and charitable. A knight was also expected to defend his church and his Christian faith. Not all knights during the Crusades belonged to orders; many fought for their feudal lords. It was assumed that if their lord joined an order, they would follow. During this time, knights were also encouraged to be ferocious in battles against the "infidels" and to always fight on the side of good and justice in defense of their people, the Christian faith, and their country.

The Legend of King Arthur

Today, many consider the fables of King Arthur and the Knights of the Round Table as nothing more than a fairytale, a legend that personifies the very idea of chivalry and bravery. Some might be surprised to learn that there was a King Arthur, and legends of this king and his brave knights were written about and respected throughout the medieval ages.

By the 11th century, the tales of King Arthur and his knights were popularly known, and in the 12th century, many sought his burial place on the island of fictional Avalon, believed to be an island in the sea just off the Cornwall coast, more commonly known as St. Michael's Mount, or perhaps a small island off the coast of Brittany. Very early in the 11th century, it was believed that Avalon was actually Glastonbury Tor, a hill near Somerset.

Rumors abound regarding King Arthur's final resting place, but today's historians believe that the actual King Arthur of legend might have been a Welsh prince who lived during the 5th or 6th century. The name Arthur is found in numerous accounts throughout the Middle Ages, harking back to the years of the many battles with the Saxons in the early decades of the 6th century.

Others believe that King Arthur was nothing more than a legend, a figure that encompassed the characteristics of soldiers at the time, and from there, the Arthurian legend was born, primarily following the publication of Geoffrey of Monmouth's *History of the Kings of Britain* around 1135.

By the year 1155, King Arthur's legend had grown, and his exploits were translated into French, with the French being among the first to define the Knights of the Round Table. One of the fictionalized accounts of Arthur's life, written by a French author, mentions a quest for the Holy Grail, the cup Christ is believed to have used during the Last Supper with his disciples. Allegedly, the cup was given to Joseph of Arimathea, who later brought the cup with him to Europe.

It was from these legends that the concept of knights living by a code of chivalry was born, as were the legends of his Knights of the Round Table, among them Sir Tristan, Sir Lancelot, Sir Galahad, and Sir Percival. All of these knights convey highly sought-after and honored qualities of knighthood, including their spirituality. During the Middle Ages, the symbolism of the Holy Grail was transformed into a literal object, a cup carefully guarded by what were known as Grail Knights or Grail Keepers, men who had been tasked with the lone objective of protecting the Holy Grail through the ages.

The ideals of honor, devotion, and dedication endured over the years as the concept of chivalry and knighthood evolved. Christian knights engaging in holy battles and acting as stalwart defenders of Jerusalem grew in popularity, leading to the growth of military orders. The search for King Arthur's verifiable resting place still continues today, and his legends endure, as do the histories and legends of many knightly orders.

Among these orders of knights were the Knights of the Holy Sepulchre, the Knights Hospitaller, the Order of St. Lazarus, and, perhaps the most well-known knightly societies in history, the Knights Templar and the Teutonic Knights.

Chapter 4 – The Knights Hospitaller

The cross of the Knights Hospitaller.
https://en.wikipedia.org/wiki/File:Cross_of_the_Knights_Hospitaller.svg

A relatively lesser-known society of knights, at least in comparison with the larger, more well-known Knights Templar, was the Knights Hospitaller. This order consisted, for the most part, of single men who adopted an almost monastic way of life.

Many of them were monks and closely adhered to that way of life. They were typically simple men with strong beliefs. Some were illiterate, while others were educated. Regardless of their education, they devoted themselves and often sacrificed their lives in their service to the order.

Clothing of the Knights Hospitaller.
https://commons.wikimedia.org/wiki/File:Chevalier_de_Rhodes,_en_habit_religieux_(XVe_siec le)_et_en_armure_(XIVe_siecle),_d%27apres_des_pierres_tombales.jpg

While knights have a reputation for being noble warriors, many of the Hospitallers were not trained in war, nor did all of them come from royal lineages or places of wealth. They did not expect a comfortable existence and were often required to journey to places that were far from comfortable, safe, or even healthy.

These warrior monks lived by extremely strict rules, even limiting the number of days they were allowed to eat meat and then only to keep up their strength. The brotherhood required them to maintain silence during meal times, and some groups were not allowed to hunt. They were expected to don plain clothing made of wool. During their leisure time, they attended services, while the more literate among them led daily prayers or services. Others served as chaplains. They were all required to recite the Lord's Prayer—the *Pater Noster*—at certain times of the day. The rules were strict, and penalties for disobedience could be severe, from a beating to performing penance.

Though most came from humble beginnings, the ranks of the Knights Hospitaller were well respected. These knights earned their reputation and the respect of their peers and contemporaries. They were known for being highly disciplined and ferocious in battle and believed they were fighting for their own salvation. However, their origins were not steeped in blood on the battlefield; rather, they began as an order that sought to help pilgrims reach the Holy Land.

The Knights Hospitaller was founded sometime between 1070 and 1080. They eventually became known as the Knights of the Order of the Hospital of St. John of Jerusalem during the later years of the First Crusade and actually received the backing of Pope Paschal II in 1113.

One branch of the Knights Hospitaller that influenced history was the Knights of St. Thomas, formally known as the Hospitallers of St. Thomas of Canterbury at Acre. They made a name for themselves during the siege of Acre in 1191. This military order was only open to Englishmen, and their patron saint was Saint Thomas Becket of Canterbury.

Thomas Becket, an English archbishop, was murdered in Canterbury Cathedral in 1170, primarily because he had gained a reputation for being a somewhat rebellious priest. His reputation was garnered after he and King Henry II experienced differences of opinion when it came to the privileges of clerics. Tensions rose when Becket insisted that the church was not to be held to the English laws of the land.

Becket, who was initially the archdeacon of Canterbury, became lord chancellor in 1155. He served the crown as a diplomat and served the king. He even acted like a soldier at times, leading troops in France to reclaim the lands of Eleanor of Aquitaine, the king's wife.

Becket was ordained as a priest, and by 1162, the year he became archbishop of Canterbury, a number of disagreements and differences of opinion between Becket and the king had come to a head, not only regarding religious disagreements but also over political issues, including taxation and the responsibilities and rights of the church in general. Their differences convinced Becket to flee to France in 1164, and he did not return until early December 1170.

The history that follows is complicated, but eventually, after some of the dust settled, Becket returned to Canterbury Cathedral while King Henry was in Normandy. Apparently, the king was outraged by this and muttered a number of unfortunate words that were heard by some knights, something along the lines of when he might be relieved of the troublesome priest.

So, Becket's fate was sealed. On December 29th, 1170, four knights (William de Tracy, Hugh de Morville, Richard le Bret, and Reginald FitzUrse) took it upon themselves to provide a solution, and Becket was violently murdered in the cathedral. Within days, Pope Alexander III canonized Becket, and he became Saint Thomas.

The incident immediately gained Becket the sympathy of Christians throughout Europe, and he was deemed a martyr. In 1174, King Henry II was absolved of the incident after doing penance at Canterbury.

It is said that some routes the pilgrims took from various parts of England to Canterbury to honor the man can still be found at the location of where his shrine once stood until it was destroyed during the Reformation.

Origins

But how did they start? Well, the Knights Hospitallers can trace their origins further than the other orders, although they weren't officially established as a military order until 1099. The original hospital was founded by Italian merchants around 1023 to take care of the poor and sick. At that time, the hospital was manned by Benedictine monks who provided shelter for religious pilgrims who made their way to Jerusalem. This hospital was believed to be on the site of a church that was linked to the Apostle John, not far from the Holy Sepulchre.

Most scholars date the knight's origins to 1099, when the Benedictine monk Blessed Gerard founded the order. Others date the origin of the order much earlier to 1080 or even earlier to the time of the aforementioned Italian merchants from Amalfi.

The Hospitallers were officially known as the Order of Knights of the Hospital of St. John of Jerusalem. However, the hospital had existed long before they came around, even before the Italian merchants rebuilt it. The first known account of a hospital in Jerusalem was in 603 when Pope Gregory I commissioned a hospital to be built. However, in 1009, the structure was destroyed by the sixth caliph of Egypt, who deliberately ordered the destruction of many Christian shrines, including the Church of the Holy Sepulchre, which was built on the site believed to be where Jesus was crucified and buried. The hospital was rebuilt by the Italian merchants in 1023.

While there are disagreements over the exact timeframe of the creation of the hospitals and hospices in Jerusalem and the Hospitallers' presence there, history does confirm that they were there in the years prior to the arrival of the Knights Templar.

Suffice it to say that the hospital was devoted to providing care to traveling pilgrims. And it is fairly well agreed upon that from the time the brothers formed the order, they devoted themselves to living a life of chastity, obedience, and poverty.

Following the conquest of Jerusalem in 1099 by Christian forces, Gerard Thom (sometimes spelled Tum), a Benedictine lay brother, became the guardian of the hospital. He eventually came to be known as "Blessed Gerard" and is believed to be the founder of the Knights of St. John.

Blessed Gerard

Blessed Gerard, also known as Gérard de Martigues, was believed to have been born around 1040. History is unclear regarding his specific date of birth and birthplace, but he is believed to have been a Benedictine lay brother. The Benedictine monks were known to wear black robes and habits, giving them the nickname the Black Monks. Gerard was known to be a man of piety and practiced humility. Numerous legends have been written about the man.

As the years passed, the hospital in Jerusalem grew, and by the 1100s, the brothers cared for hundreds of patients, regardless of the religion they practiced or where they came from. Over the years, stories have been written that in times of need, the brothers would give up their beds and sleep on the floor to better care for their patients.

An image of Blessed Gerard.
https://commons.wikimedia.org/wiki/File:Gravure_de_Fra_Gerard_fondateur_des_Hospitaliers_de_Saint-Jean.jpg

Blessed Gerard was known to have traveled far and wide to gather support for the hospital and to raise money. He won over Pope Paschal II, who determined that the Order of the Hospitallers was to be subservient only to the papacy and not to the king of Jerusalem. The pope also exempted the order from paying church tithes.

Over the years, Gerard established hospitals along the routes typically taken by pilgrims to the Holy Land, and the order eventually became more than caretakers. The brothers provided pilgrimages with armed escorts along the more dangerous sections of their long journeys.

It wasn't until around 1113 that Pope Paschal II officially sanctioned the order, which was dedicated to Saint John the Baptist. At times, the hospital in Jerusalem is believed to have contained upward of two thousand patients.

Following the death of Blessed Gerard in 1120, the order slowly acquired more responsibilities in addition to taking care of the sick, and those responsibilities included military expectations. In 1121, Raymond du Puy stepped up to become the second grand master.

Note of interest: Relic

In the capital of Malta today, preserved in the convent of St. Ursula in Valletta, is a relic believed to be the skull of Blessed Gerard.

Raymond du Puy: The Second Grand Master of the Hospitaller Order (1121–1160)

Over the years following the origin of the hospital-based order that strictly followed Benedictine rules, the Hospitallers began to take on new roles. By the mid-1100s, they had been tasked to become defenders of the Holy Land. Over time, the rules regarding the behavior and actions of knightly orders changed according to circumstances, and the same is true of this order.

When Raymond du Puy, a French knight, became the second grand master of the Hospitallers around 1121, he revised expectations regarding the brotherhood. This list, called the Rule of the Order of St. John, contained the following:

1. How the brethren should make their profession
2. What the brethren should claim as their due
3. Concerning the conduct of the brethren in the service of the church and in the reception of the sick

4. How the brethren should go abroad and behave

5. By whom and how alms should be sought

6. Concerning the alms obtained in concerning the produce of the houses (they could not take land from collected alms, but they could take a third of food, including bread and wine, and the surplus could be given to the poor in Jerusalem)

7. Who and in what manner they should go abroad to preach

8. Concerning the clothing and food of the brethren

9. Concerning brethren guilty of fornication

10. Concerning brethren quarreling or striking one another

11. Concerning the silence of the brethren

12. Concerning brethren misbehaving

13. Concerning brethren found with private property

14. What office should be celebrated for the deceased brethren

15. How the things here detailed are to be firmly maintained

16. How our lords the sick should be received and served

17. In what manner brethren may correct brethren

18. How one brother should accuse another brother

19. That the brethren bear on their breasts the sign of the cross

A copper engraving of Raymond du Puy by Laurent Cars.
https://commons.wikimedia.org/wiki/File:%2BRaymond_du_Puy,_by_Laurent_Cars.jpg

Raymond du Puy guided the Hospitallers to become a group of brothers dedicated to providing for the sick, defending the faith, and fighting infidels. The eight-pointed star they wore on their robes symbolized their pledge to give their lives to their faith and to Christ and to follow the example of the martyrs who came before them.

The Hospitallers took part in battles in current-day Palestine and other places in the Holy Land, and they fought alongside other crusaders and mercenaries. It is said the Hospitallers were rarely captured as prisoners since there was no point in trying to ransom them or release them by encouraging them to deny Christ.

While Raymond du Puy was known as a devoted Christian and crusader, he was also known to be sensible and did not encourage wanton destruction in the aftermath of battles.

Several paintings depicting Raymond du Puy exist in Malta. There are also paintings of other saints of the order, including Blessed Gerard, in Valletta. (The painting of Saint John by Caravaggio in 1608 is also there.)

Raymond du Puy died around 1160 after leading the Hospitallers as their second grand master for thirty-three years.

What Happened to the Hospitallers?

Following the deaths of Blessed Gerard and Raymond du Puy, other grand masters stepped up to lead the order, first in Jerusalem until approximately 1187, after the city fell once again to the Muslims, then to Margat, and then to Acre in 1191. After the fall of Acre in 1291, they left the Holy Land and relocated to Cyprus, but the terrain wasn't fruitful enough to support them, so they relocated to Rhodes, which they were forced to take from the Byzantines. The Hospitallers ruled Rhodes from 1309 to 1522.

While their numbers rarely exceeded several hundred knights in the crusading armies, they were credited with aiding the evacuation of Acre in 1291 and protecting refugees escaping to Cyprus. They served as knights and medics on the battlefield.

In later years, they engaged in several campaigns in battles over the Ottoman Empire. The Hospitallers were part of the capture of Izmir in 1344 and took part in the attack on Alexandria in 1365.

The Hospitallers remained in Rhodes for just over two centuries until 1522, when they relocated to the island of Malta, where they remained until the late 18th century. In 1834, they became a permanent fixture of Rome.

Today, the eightieth grand master of the Sovereign Military and Hospitaller Order of St. John of Jerusalem of Rhodes and of Malta (the Order of Malta, for short) resides over the order, which today is recognized as a religious order of the Roman Catholic Church, as well as a sovereign one according to international law. The order is still dedicated to helping the poor and defending the Christian faith. Today, the Order of Malta continues to maintain diplomatic associations and relationships with the Holy See and seventy-five other countries around the world.

Through the 1990s, membership required proof of noble lineage, but today, the order focuses primarily on international and humanitarian issues around the globe. They provide relief, aid, and support to the less fortunate, as well as aiding in natural disasters and providing support to countries devastated by war and epidemics. Today, members of the order focus on the pursuit of their humanitarian services, though they still wear white shirts with the emblem of a red shield with a white eight-pointed cross or similar emblems.

Chapter 5 – The Knights of the Holy Sepulchre

The coat of arms of the Knights of the Holy Sepulchre.

Mathieu CHAINE, CC BY-SA 3.0 <https://creativecommons.org/licenses/by-sa/3.0>, via Wikimedia Commons; https://commons.wikimedia.org/wiki/File:GA_Ordre_du_Saint-S%C3%A9pulcre.svg

The Knights of the Holy Sepulchre was formed to protect the tomb of Christ in the Holy City, also known as Jerusalem. However, their story is perhaps not as well known as the other military orders, such as the Knights Templar, though their loyalty and devotion to their task were equal to none.

The historical origins of the Knights of the Holy Sepulchre differ slightly, as many of the histories and traditions of the order were passed down orally. However, the order is believed to have been founded during the First Crusade with the capture of Jerusalem in 1099.

Origins of the Knights of the Holy Sepulchre

The Knights of the Holy Sepulchre was conceived as an order under the leadership of a man named Godfrey of Bouillon, who is credited with helping to capture Jerusalem during the First Crusade (1096–1099), the first of many religious wars.

However, some historians trace the order as far back as decades after the crucifixion and death of Jesus Christ, with the order being tasked to protect his tomb. As one might expect, the history of the Knights of the Holy Sepulchre is bound up in legend and traditions that go back in time before Godfrey of Bouillon, stretching back as far as the first bishop of Jerusalem himself, Saint James the Just.

First Crusader Warrior: Godfrey of Bouillon

Godfrey of Bouillon hailed from France and was born around 1060. He was not only a nobleman but also a valiant leader during the First Crusade. Godfrey actually became the first ruler of Jerusalem, serving in that role from 1099 to 1100. He didn't want to be called a king; instead, he preferred to be called "an advocate of the Holy Sepulchre."

Godfrey's early history is mired in the vagueness of legends. However, by the age of forty, he took up the cross, something that nobles throughout the land were urged to do during the First Crusade. At the time, many nobles willingly joined, not only for religious reasons but also to procure lands or other material resources.

Statue of Godfrey of Bouillon, Brussels
https://en.wikipedia.org/wiki/File:Godefroy.jpg

During the First Crusade, Godfrey of Bouillon and his two brothers, Baldwin and Eustace III, Count of Boulogne, commanded a contingent of approximately forty thousand men (approximately ten thousand knights and thirty thousand foot soldiers) that set out from the area of Lorraine in northern France.

During the late summer of 1096, Bouillon and his men set out for Constantinople, taking a route that many pilgrims had taken before him through what is known as present-day Hungary and the Balkans, though at the time, it was known as the Byzantine Empire.

Godfrey of Bouillon partook in the siege of Antioch and then proceeded to Edessa. Legend has it that he prompted over 150 Turks to flee with only a dozen knights. He could reputedly cut a Turkish horseman in half with one mighty sweep of his sword.

In 1098, Godfrey of Bouillon journeyed to Jerusalem, arriving there in the early summer of 1099, though according to some sources, he lost nearly ninety percent of his men en route. He and his men were active in the siege of the Holy City. He is reputed to be among the first to enter the city, along with his brother Eustace, in mid-July of that year. According to legend, he made a vow (which he kept) following his entry into the city. It is said that he put down his arms and, wearing only his undergarments, rounded the ramparts of the city and then went to pray at the site of the Holy Sepulchre.

Godfrey was suggested to become and was ultimately elected the king of Jerusalem, although he refused to wear a crown, claiming that he refused to do so out of respect for Christ, who had been crowned in that very place with a crown of thorns. Godfrey accepted the position solely for his love of Christ.

It was Godfrey's responsibility to ensure the safety and survival of this new kingdom, which was a very uncertain prospect at the time, especially after a great bulk of the crusaders who had journeyed and fought with him eventually returned home. It is said that he was left with perhaps three hundred knights, a couple thousand infantry footmen, and no ships with which he could defend the city. A heavy burden had been placed on his shoulders, yet he managed to negotiate a number of treaties and truces with many surrounding cities and especially after defeating the Egyptian army in the Battle of Ascalon. The battle occurred in August of 1099, barely a month after he succeeded in capturing Jerusalem.

At the time, the secular order of the Knights of the Holy Sepulchre was charged with the protection of the holiest places of Jerusalem, including the tomb of Christ. It was not so much by design but rather a sense of duty that the knights in charge of defending the Holy Sepulchre became known as such. Therefore, it can be assumed that any knight who took up the sword in defense of such holy sites also took upon the identity of being a part of the Knights of the Holy Sepulchre.

Godfrey of Bouillon made a name for himself in history, as he was respected by many as a true protector of the church. Historical accounts of his demise differ, with some claiming that Godfrey fell victim to the plague in Caesarea not long before reaching Jerusalem the previous June. He never fully recovered and passed away in mid-July in 1100. Others claim that he had been struck by an arrow during the siege of Acre and endured an infection that gradually seeped into his bloodstream and eventually caused his death. Some accounts even propose that he had been poisoned by the emir of Caesarea.

Before Godfrey died, he named his brother Baldwin as his successor. He was buried in the Church of the Holy Sepulchre. Yet his legend continued to grow.

Following his death, Godfrey of Bouillon was portrayed as the epitome of a medieval knight. According to historical documents, he was similar to what the legends claimed: a man of courage, a Christian knight, tall, handsome, and courteous. He kept to his vows without question and at great personal cost.

Although Godfrey of Bouillon was among the first Christians to step into Jerusalem that July in 1099, he did not have long to enjoy the success of his long and arduous journey. However, he left behind a legacy of dedication and determination. Within one hundred years of his passing, Godfrey became a hero, and stories about him were told throughout the noble courts.

While myth and legend often develop about heroes and leaders of the past, it is important to remember, especially as it pertains to Godfrey of Bouillon, that he was a simple man, a man who fought hard and bravely for what he believed in. Whether all the stories passed down over the ages about him are true, one thing cannot be denied. He is still known as the defender of the Holy Sepulchre, and he certainly carried great influence and had an even greater impact on history, as he was the Christian knight who helped take back Jerusalem and become the first overseer of the Kingdom of Jerusalem.

The tomb of Christ continues to be a holy site, and pilgrimages to the believed site of the Holy Sepulchre have endured throughout the centuries.

Note of Interest: Godfrey of Bouillon and the Nine Worthies

Throughout the ages, civilization has often turned its attention to the "greats" of their times, such as the Seven Wonders of the Ancient World or the best fast-food places. During the Middle Ages, one of the most interesting of these lists was called the Nine Worthies. These are men who were purported to have been the most chivalrous and brave in all of history. These men were believed to have exemplified idealized virtues, especially dedication, loyalty, and service to their country and faith.

During the Middle Ages, this list included three Christians, three Jews, and three pagans. It is believed that each set symbolized aspects of heroism, devotion, and loyalty during the development of the concept of chivalry, as well as exemplified the efforts of mankind to accept and spread the divine will of God.

The three Jewish worthies are found in the Old Testament of the Holy Bible: David, Joshua, and Judas Maccabeus. Joshua became the leader of the Jews after the death of Moses. He was perceived as a general of the Israelites, who eventually conquered the Holy Land. David, the boy who fought Goliath and won, became the "anointed" man of God's family line and was instructed by God to lead his people to freedom and faith. Judas Maccabeus was a priest who ultimately led the Maccabees in a revolt against the Seleucid Empire to resist the spread of Hellenism in Judea and preserve the Jewish religion. He restored worship at the Temple of Jerusalem, which is still celebrated as Hanukkah every year.

Three pagan worthies were also recognized, among them Alexander the Great, Hector, and Julius Caesar, who represented Roman or pagan laws. Hector, a prince and also one of Troy's heroes, fought to defend his homeland, while Alexander the Great is no stranger to historians around the world. This great general is recognized as spreading Greek knowledge and wisdom throughout the Mediterranean and Persian regions. Julius Caesar was one of the most well-known rulers of Rome and sought to encourage peace

---

following his conquests.

Three Christian worthies are recognized, including King Arthur, Charlemagne, and Godfrey of Bouillon. Perhaps combining fact and fiction, the legend of King Arthur and the concept of chivalry and his knights continue to this day, as he is known for his honor and desire to spread Christianity. As for Charlemagne, he is credited with the origin of the Holy Roman Empire and was crowned its king circa 800 CE. Charlemagne was known as the man who protected Christians and Christianity, especially the Roman papacy.

Godfrey of Bouillon was a contemporary of the Middle Ages, a French knight who led the First Crusade into the Holy Land and who became the brief ruler of the Kingdom of Jerusalem before his untimely death a mere year later. Godfrey epitomized the concept of the divine mission of chivalry, a mission that has endured for centuries and continues to this day.

What Happened to the Order of the Knights of the Holy Sepulchre?

The Order of the Knights of the Holy Sepulchre still exists today. It is one of the oldest orders in Catholic history. These knights may no longer wear the armor that they used to, but they continue to dedicate and devote themselves to the honor and preservation of the tomb of Christ in the city of Jerusalem.

In the 13th century, the Order of the Knights of the Holy Sepulchre was led by Franciscan missionaries. They were charged with maintaining the holy sites and establishing and protecting churches, hospitals, schools, and convents in the Holy Land. By the mid-1840s, the Latin patriarchate of Jerusalem, which was reestablished by Pope Pius IX, basically relieved the Franciscans of their duties.

Around 1496, the grand masters of the Order of the Holy Sepulchre were vested in the papacy. Just after the turn of the 20th century, in 1906, Pope Pius X took the role of grand master, and since then, the order has maintained four primary types of memberships, including knight, commander, commander with a star, and knight with a grand cross. Membership requires each of these knights to protect the tomb of Christ and other holy sites in Jerusalem. Since 1949, grand masters of the order have been cardinals and, as such, remain in their headquarters in Rome.

So, from the First Crusade until today, the Order of the Knights of the Holy Sepulchre is still devoted and dedicated to the protection and preservation of historical sites in the Holy City.

Chapter 6 – The Order of St. Lazarus

The flag of the Order of St. Lazarus.
https://commons.wikimedia.org/wiki/File:Flag_of_the_Order_of_Saint_Lazarus.svg

Another lesser-known order of knights during the medieval ages was the Order of St. Lazarus of Jerusalem, which was founded around 1119, although some historians claim that the order was established around 1123. Regardless, this order was small; it was certainly smaller than the Knights Hospitaller, the Teutonic Knights, and the Knights Templar. Its mission was not all that unique from the other orders, as its members were also dedicated to caring for the pilgrims and soldiers who ventured to the Holy City, but the order was known for something unique.

The Order of St. Lazarus was dedicated to caring for lepers. In the Middle Ages, leprosy was greatly feared. Anyone who contracted it was literally shunned and driven from the community. In fact, any Knights Templar who contracted the dreaded wasting disease was required by Templar rules to transfer immediately into the Order of St. Lazarus. It is believed that the Templars helped train the medically focused brothers in the ways of the military.

Leprosy during the Middle Ages

From about the 11th to the 14th century, leprosy was a fairly common disease throughout Europe and the Middle East. It struck individuals of all ages and from all aspects of society, regardless of religion, country of origin, or status. There was no cure for leprosy at the time, and the disease carried a huge social stigma and prejudice. The disease physically alters human flesh, so back in the Middle Ages, it was believed that the disease was a punishment from God.

Lepers were greatly feared. They were outcasts, isolated and destined to live lonely and poverty-stricken lives until they died. Today, we know that leprosy is caused by a bacterium called *Mycobacterium leprae*, yet such knowledge was centuries away back in the medieval period. Those who contracted leprosy during the Middle Ages endured terrible changes to their bodies, especially their skin and eyes. Leprosy damages the inner organs and nerves and, in severe cases, causes facial and bodily malformations and transfigurations.

Leprosy has existed for millennia. The first mention of it has been found in the land known as India today, dating back to the year 2000 BCE, and it has also been written about in ancient Chinese and Egyptian writings. Documents talk of the existence of leprosy in the ancient kingdoms of Africa as well.

In the medieval ages, it was believed that leprosy first made an appearance in the Mediterranean region of Europe by troops led by King Alexander the Great. It was thought that the scourge might have been brought from India and then through Egypt around the 5th century BCE. However, references to leprosy are also found in the Old Testament and in the texts of Aristotle and Hippocrates, although the first detailed description of the disease was written by a Greek physician named Aretaeus in about 150 CE.

The existence of leprosy is an important aspect of the history of the Order of St. Lazarus, and the fear and stigma of this disease during the

Middle Ages cannot be overemphasized. Many people from numerous countries were terrified of the disease, which makes it even more impressive that the brothers of the Order of St. Lazarus dedicated their lives to providing aid and succor to individuals afflicted by it.

It is for this reason that the Order of St. Lazarus of Jerusalem came to be known as the "Leper Brothers" following its founding of a hospital for lepers around 1119. According to some sources, the founders of the order were knights suffering from leprosy and dedicated themselves and their order to care for those with the dreaded disease. Their patron saint was and continues to be Lazarus, who was raised from the dead by Christ in the Holy Bible.

It wasn't until 1255 that the Order of St. Lazarus gained the recognition of the papacy under the reign of Pope Alexander IV and enjoyed many of the same privileges as other knightly orders before them. The order received gifts of endowments from a number of European kings and emperors, including Louis VII of France, Holy Roman Emperor Frederick II, and King Henry II of England.

Historically, it is believed that the numbers of the Order of St. Lazarus grew, especially after 1262, when Pope Clement IV ordered priests to "confine" any leper (regardless of whether they were a man, woman, child, or layman) to the leper houses of St. Lazarus. Throughout these years, more than one leper house existed. Hundreds of them sprung up throughout Europe during the Middle Ages.

Over the years, the order became more militarized. Its brothers were likely trained by the Templars. However, the order's history is convoluted. Following the defeat of Jerusalem in 1187, the Order of St. Lazarus relocated to Acre, just as the Hospitallers before them. While they were known to engage in a few battles, such as the Battle of La Forbie (1244) and the Battle of Mansurah (1250), they were primarily known as a monastic military brotherhood after the fall of Acre in 1291, even though they had gained a reputation for being fierce warriors in battle and a trained force of highly disciplined men.

What Happened to the Order of St. Lazarus?

The historical timeline of the Order of St. Lazarus of Jerusalem provides a fascinating glimpse into the history of the times, especially in regard to the fear of lepers and their isolation, as well as the dedication of those who cared for them. While it is believed that the leper hospital in Jerusalem was founded sometime after 1098 and provided care to lepers in the Holy Land before the First Crusade, they didn't become known as a military order until later, taking part in some battles during the Second Crusade. In 1191, the leper hospital in Jerusalem was abandoned, and they maintained a new home base in Acre.

Approximately fifty years later, the order's historical timeline states that its men fought in the Battle of Gaza in 1244, where all the leper knights were killed. Throughout the decades, they continued to participate in a number of clashes until 1291. It has been said that all members of the order were killed in the unsuccessful defense of Acre.

Yet the Order of St. Lazarus survived to a certain extent, though by the mid-1400s, their raison d'être had faded since the scourge of leprosy was declining. Like the Knights of the Holy Sepulchre and even the Hospitallers, the Order of St. Lazarus faded somewhat, at least in their actions and reputations as mighty knights. However, new eras saw the order working quietly to support the sick and needy. Today, it continues to provide humanitarian and philanthropic aid around the globe.

Following the French Revolution, chivalric orders no longer enjoyed legalized recognition in France. The 1920s saw the reorganization of the former order, and in 1927, it was reorganized as the *Association Française des Hospitaliers de Saint-Lazare de Jérusalem*. In 1929, the order's statutes and rules were based on the 1841 Fundamental Statute of the Knights Hospitaller.

The Order of St. Lazarus of Jerusalem still exists today and is unique among the many Catholic orders since it allows non-Catholic members. The order has maintained a spirit of service, morality, discipline, and sacrifice that exemplify the knights of old and their dedication to helping others.

Today, the military and hospital order continues to focus on and care for members of society, including those living in poverty and the homeless. It claims to be an apolitical and non-denominational organization, with roughly four thousand members located across five continents, making it the smallest of the medieval military orders today. The organization continues to make pilgrimages to the Holy Land and dedicates itself to maintaining the history and purpose of the order.

Chapter 7 – The Teutonic Knights

The coat of arms of the Teutonic Knights.

While it is often assumed that many of the orders of knights were English, several come to mind that were not. For instance, the Teutonic Knights were primarily of Germanic origin.

The Third Crusade was initiated by Pope Gregory VIII after the capture of Jerusalem by Saladin in 1187. For the most part, the crusade was composed of European nobility, but it was nearly abandoned following the drowning of the king of Germany and Holy Roman emperor, Frederick I Barbarossa, in 1190. Many of his troops, disheartened and grieving, returned to their native land, but others continued to partake in the siege of Acre, which concluded in the mid-summer of 1191.

While the crusaders recaptured a number of cities throughout the region, Jerusalem was not destined to be one of them. In 1191, after the crusaders gained Acre, German merchants traveled to the city, where they established a hospital to provide care for those living there. They began calling it the Hospital of St. Mary of the German House in Jerusalem. The pope approved of the order, and thus, the Teutonic Knights were born.

The Teutonic Order can be defined as a type of Hospitaller order due to their original purpose in establishing the hospital. However, the Teutonic Order was independent of the Hospitallers. The primary focus of the Teutonic Knights' mission can be defined as "recapturing" stolen lands, not so much the conversion of the Arabs to Christianity. So, the Teutonic Knights and their goals differed from other orders that came before them.

Despite numerous attempts, the conquest of the volatile territories of the Middle East proved elusive, and the Teutonic Knights refocused their efforts toward the central and eastern portions of Europe, which eventually became known as Prussia. They were determined to convert the pagans to Christianity and accumulate more lands.

In their early years, the Teutonic Knights were accepted as a monastic brotherhood by the pope as simple men of simple means, but in 1198, with the approval of King Amalric II of Jerusalem, they were also recognized as a military order.

At the time of this recognition, approximately forty knights were inducted into the new order, and Heinrich Walpot von Bassenheim was made its first grand master. The primary requirement of knights in this fraternity mandated that they be of German birth, which made it unusual from other orders that had been founded in the Holy Land. Most of those knights came from noble classes or were related to other knights.

The Teutonic Knights were easily recognized by their white tunics or cloaks emblazoned with a black cross, and the Germanic brotherhood made their organization similar to that of the Knights Templar.

However, the Teutonic Knights were not nearly as large as the Hospitaller or Templar orders, but if one thing could be said of them, it was that they were intimidating, at least in regard to their power. As time passed, the Teutonic Knights became known as clever traders and political diplomats, with their reputation and control reaching from Prussia throughout Europe and as far as Sicily to the south and Lithuania to the east.

The First Grand Master

The first grand master of the Teutonic Knights was Heinrich Walpot von Bassenheim. He only served for a couple of years, from 1198 to 1200. Little is known about the man. It is believed he was born sometime between 1074 and 1094, although his date of death is unknown. Much of the history surrounding the man consists of myth, supposition, and plain old-fashioned guesswork. However, it is believed that he came from a rich family in the area of Mainz, and he is given credit for transforming the brotherhood into a military order.

It is believed that around 1199, he received a set of monastery rules from the grand master of the Knights Templar at the request of Pope Innocent III.

The grand master divided his knights into two primary classes: priests and simple knights. The knights were required to take vows, as other orders did at the time, of chastity, poverty, and obedience, as well as a dedication to fighting infidels and providing aid to the sick. However, and somewhat unusually, contrary to other orders of the time, the priests were *only* obligated to oversee and celebrate religious offices, such as administering the sacrament to the sick while they were in the hospital and to the knights themselves.

The priests were not allowed, at least in Lithuania or Prussia, to become commanders or masters of the military, although they were allowed to become commanders in their native land of Germany.

Brief Timeline of the Teutonic Knights

Following the death of Heinrich Walpot von Bassenheim, the Teutonic Order was led by Otto von Kerpen, who hailed from Bremen. However, it wasn't until around 1210, during the leadership of the fourth grand master, Herman von Salza, that the order's respectability and prestige were enhanced. Due to his ability to maintain peace between Holy Roman Emperor Frederick II and Pope Gregory IX in

1230, he gained the respect and trust of both, which led to an increase in wealth and possessions, including lands.

From about 1210 to 1239, the lives and struggles of the brotherhood of Germanic knights were by no means easy or without strife. Following the siege of Acre in the Third Crusade, the order turned its attention from the Middle East to central and eastern Europe. The Teutonic Knights' first forays into eastern Europe took them to Hungary in 1211 when King Andrew II asked them to help protect his Transylvanian borders and push back incursions by the nomadic Turks.

However, things didn't go so well for the Teutonic Knights in Hungary, especially after von Salza tried to gain authority and establish his own independent principality rather than following the Hungarian king. They were ultimately expelled from those lands in 1225.

Undaunted, the Teutonic Order persisted in its efforts to convert pagans to Christianity throughout the lands of central and eastern Europe. In 1226, under Herman von Salza, the knights agreed to fight against the pagan Prussians pushing against the borders of Poland. The bad blood between the Prussians and the Poles had been prevalent since 1221, when the Prussians launched their first crusade against Poland. Conrad of Mazovia, a Polish duke, requested the aid of the Teutonic Knights in controlling the pagan Prussians pushing at his borders. In 1233, the order proceeded with their intended conquest of Prussia.

In 1260, at the Battle of Durbe, the Teutonic Knights suffered a crushing loss, but they held out in the region while waiting for reinforcements, which didn't arrive until 1265. The Prussians were fairly unorganized and didn't take advantage of their position, nor did they have a strategy to use. Following the arrival of reinforcements, the Teutonic Knights pressed their advantage and came out victorious by 1274. By 1283, the knights had gained control over much of Prussia.

For nearly five decades, the Teutonic Knights fought, battled, and continually sought to convert the pagans to Christianity, and they primarily governed through pressure. In the intervening years, they built several fortress settlements, including one in Königsberg, which is now located in present-day Russia but at that time lay between Lithuania and Poland. Several other settlements were formed, but the conflicts between the Prussians and the Teutonic Order continued, with claims of brutality and torture on both sides.

During these years, the influence of the Teutonic Knights grew throughout Europe, including the outer regions of eastern Europe (Romania at the time), Greece, and the outer edges of the Byzantine Empire. Numerous estates were given to the Teutonic Knights for their services, reaching as far north as the Netherlands and down into the lands of France and even as far south as Sicily and then eastward into Prussia.

Throughout the years of the early 13th century, the Teutonic Knights built numerous castles throughout the Middle East, as their main mission was to maintain and defend lands and fortifications that had been gained in previous years.

However, conflicts eventually arose between the Knights Templar and the Teutonic Knights, the latter of which made their headquarters at Montfort Castle in the northern region of present-day Israel in about 1220. The castle was located along the road between the eastern coastline of the Mediterranean and Jerusalem. By 1229, Montfort Castle was considered the home base of the grand masters of the Teutonic Order, as well as a place to store its archives and treasures.

During the beginning and middle of the 13th century, the entirety of Europe was under threat of Mongol invasions. By 1240, a huge swathe of the populace had been overrun by the Mongols. But despite the need for a united front against the Mongols, disagreements and infighting among the Teutonic Knights and the general populations of the lands they sought to control occurred.

At the same time, the Teutonic Knights made several attempts to expand their influence eastward, hoping to convert the Russians to the Roman Catholic faith. However, they were roundly defeated at the Battle on the Ice in 1242. The Teutonic Knights faced off against Alexander Nevsky, who is seen as one of the most important medieval figures in Russian history.

It was not an easy life for the Teutonic Knights. In 1244, Jerusalem fell into the hands of the Ayyubids of Egypt. In the Battle of La Forbie (located near Gaza), it is believed that approximately 437 Teutonic Knights were killed out of a force of 440. Over time, their forces were replenished, but the fighting was not over.

The knights repeatedly came under attack by the Mamluk sultan, Baybars. After initially driving him back, the knights found themselves once again fighting him five years later, in 1271. And after a week-long siege, the knights surrendered their castle at Montfort and returned to Acre.

Around 1283, the Teutonic Order primarily ruled from Prussia, where they had succeeded in converting a large number of the inhabitants of those lands to Christianity. However, their need for soldiers became desperate. They began to conscript locals, which ultimately led to rebellions against the Teutonic Knights, as the people resented their presence and demands that they convert to Christianity. In some cases, knights captured by the locals in the land now known as Lithuania were executed.

As such, by the time of the fall of Acre in 1291, the Teutonic Knights were not as strong as they should have been. They were forced to retreat to Cyprus and then to Venice, where they briefly regrouped before the brotherhood was again torn from within by quarrels and differences of opinion. The following centuries offered few victories for the Teutonic Knights, and they lost much of their autonomy.

Some historical writings claim that the knights often behaved unchristian-like. There were claims that the knights slaughtered Christians, ruined secular churches, engaged in trade with heathens, and interfered with conversions to Christianity. It is believed that many of the non-Christians in the region resisted conversion to Christianity because they didn't want to live under the control of the Teutonic Knights.

An investigation of their behavior was initiated by the pope in 1310, but nothing came of it, and it was ultimately determined that the rumors were being spread by enemies of the Teutonic Order.

Grand Master Conrad von Feuchtwangen ordered the Teutonic Knights to relocate to Venice, Italy, after the fall of Acre in 1291. In 1309, Grand Master Siegfried von Feuchtwangen (a relative of Conrad) again ordered them to relocate, this time to Poland and Malbork Castle. The order was successful in defending the castle after a two-month-long siege from Polish and Lithuanian forces, avoiding annihilation.

In 1386, one of Lithuania's dukes (Grand Duke Jogaila) was converted and baptized as a Roman Catholic Christian, and he married Poland's queen, automatically advancing him to the role of king. However, this union combined the forces of Lithuania and Poland at the time, creating a united force that threatened the Teutonic Knights and their control over the land.

At the same time, conversion to Christianity spread throughout Lithuania and Prussia, which didn't stop the bickering and feuds with Poland and Lithuania.

The knights also continued their conflicts against Poland. Even though the country converted to Christianity around 1387, the Lithuanians and the Poles united their forces and battled the Teutonic Knights a mere twenty-three years later and defeated them at the Battle of Grunwald during the Polish-Lithuanian-Teutonic War. Ultimately, the Germanic brotherhood conceded the territory to Poland.

By that point, a grand master of the order, Ulrich von Jungingen, and many of the order's higher-ranking members had been severely wounded or killed on the battlefield, leaving only a handful of the order standing.

A peace treaty was signed in 1411. While the Teutonic Order was able to retain much of its currently held territories, its reputation as nearly indestructible soldiers and knights was forever put to rest.

The Influence of the Teutonic Knights

The Teutonic Knights often came from noble or aristocratic families, with their numbers varying in size over the years. However, many of them joined for a sense of camaraderie of a specific purpose, food and shelter, a thirst for adventure, and ambition.

The number of men serving the Teutonic Knights was fluid and really depended on the political atmosphere of the time. All in all, it was considered a relatively small order, which history believes averaged no more than 1,300 men at any given time.

The Teutonic Knights followed the basic guidelines of other monastic orders, taking vows of obedience, chastity, and poverty, although many of them, like the other knightly orders, hoped that their services in the name of God, Christianity, and honor would gain them rewards, not only in the near future but also after they died.

The order, particularly at Malbork, created what can be likened today as a half-convent, half-castle, with soldiers, civilians, and others of non-combatant status relegated to serving as craftsmen and servants, otherwise providing the knights their daily needs, which included food, shelter, clothing, and so forth.

The men serving in the Teutonic brotherhood of knights benefited from booty taken from captured territories, including weapons, armor, and livestock. However, the Germanic knights primarily made a name for themselves as being excellent traders. In times of relative stability, they became landlords. In times of strife, when their numbers were large enough, they took on mercenaries, who were primarily paid by taxes incurred on local populations. As an added benefit, commanders often offered training services, shelter, and even lands where former members could live out their days.

The order wasn't only focused on war; it also created schools and hospitals. They built castles and churches. When not engaged in battle, they were required to follow a number of rules, even more so than some other military orders. They were required to maintain closely shorn hair but could grow beards. Gaudy or flamboyant equipment or clothing was discouraged. They were not allowed to display their personal coat of arms or seals and were not allowed to mingle with the knights of other orders or engage in any jousting activities or many types of hunting.

In the early decades of the 14th century, the Teutonic Knights reached the pinnacle of their power. They had supposedly (and this is still in question) been given permission by Holy Roman Emperor Louis IV to conquer the lands of Lithuania and Russian (Rus) holdings, and the Teutonic Knights gave it their best. Over the ensuing years and under the directorship of Grand Master Winrich von Kniprode (who maintained his position from 1351 to 1382), the knights made more of a name for themselves, gaining the attention of other crusaders and nobles throughout Christendom.

Changes on the Horizon

Following their failure to maintain their hold on their home base at Malbork Castle, the order disintegrated, and what followed were years of internal feuds and bickering. While the Teutonic Knights raised taxes on the lands they held, they didn't seem to have much interest in representing the populace, who held them in low esteem. Grand Master Heinrich von Plauen was forcefully removed from his position. The man who replaced him, Michael Küchmeister von Sternberg, also failed to restore order to the group. The Teutonic Knights suffered loss after loss.

As a final blow, in 1454, the Prussian Confederation rose up against the Teutonic Knights, initiating the Thirteen Years' War. Prussia wanted to get out from under the control of the Teutonic Knights. The war took a heavy toll on Prussia and the Teutonic Knights, but ultimately (and with great reluctance), the Teutonic Knights officially recognized Poland's rights over the lands of western Prussia. However, since their stronghold at Marienberg had been lost, the knights removed to Königsberg.

What followed was years of infighting and skirmishes. Throughout the centuries, the Teutonic Knights fought bravely, if somewhat recklessly. In 1525, Grand Master Elbert (Albert) of Brandenburg converted to Lutheranism, so he could no longer be a member of the order. He was succeeded by Walter von Cronberg, who became the thirty-eighth grand master of the order.

The order managed to hang on to a large number of properties in Germany, and subsequent grand masters of the order often came from noble German families. By the mid-1700s, the Teutonic Knights held lands in Bohemia, Germany, and Austria. During those years, the knights were often called upon to command groups of mercenaries during the Ottoman wars.

At the dawn of the 19th century, Napoleon seized the order's holdings and dissolved the order in 1809. Yet just a few decades later, the Teutonic Knights reemerged in Vienna, and by the early 1830s, they primarily existed as an ecclesiastical group focused on charity work.

World War II

After the Teutonic Knights were, for all intents and purposes, disbanded during Napoleon's subsequent rule, the remnants of the Teutonic Knights took up in Austria. By 1834, it had regained its official title as a *Deutcher Ritterorden*, or German knightly order, with its members overseen primarily by members of the Habsburg dynasty until 1923.

By the end of the 1920s, the former warrior order of Teutonic Knights was living a primarily spiritual life. However, by the 1930s, war was once again on the horizon, with Nazi Germany annexing Austria in 1938. Adolf Hitler ordered the Teutonic Order to be abolished, although it would rise up again after the end of the Second World War in 1945.

However, the Nazis under Adolf Hitler assumed the imagery (the black cross on a white background) for war propaganda purposes, likely to instill fear in their detractors since the Teutonic Knights had a reputation for bravery on the battlefield. The Teutonic Knights were German-based, and Hitler sought to promote German nationalism as much as he could. He also pointed to the past expansionist efforts of the Teutonic Knights, believing it gave him credence for what he was trying to do.

During the years of the Second World War, the order managed to survive in Italy, only to be reborn again in Germany and Austria following the conclusion of the war and the destruction of the Nazi Party.

What Happened to the Teutonic Knights?

Following the conclusion of the Second World War, the Teutonic Knights maintained a presence in southern Europe, although they focused on providing charity, health care, and medical services. However, by the late 1990s, numerous sponsors enabled the order to engage in a number of archaeological excavations and curiosity-seeking tourism projects throughout the Middle East.

However, by the 2000s, the German chapters of the order officially declared insolvency and disbanded.

Today, the Teutonic Knights function on a relatively small but global scale with members that include priests and nuns who are fairly localized throughout central Europe, including the Czech Republic, Slovakia, and Slovenia, as well as throughout Austria, Italy, and Germany. They focus primarily on offering spiritual guidance and medical care for the elderly and ill.

So, in the end, the Order of the Teutonic Knights returned to its origins, providing care for sojourners to the Holy Land and seeing to the spiritual need of others. Today, a museum at their former Castle in Bad Mergentheim, Germany, the home base of the grand masters from 1527 through 1809, has been dedicated to the Teutonic Knights.

Chapter 8: The Knights Templar

The cross of the Knights Templar.
https://commons.wikimedia.org/wiki/File:Knights_Templar_Cross.svg

The Knights Templar is perhaps the most well-known order of knights, although there is still an aura of mystery surrounding it. Much but not all of its history has been found in historical records of the order and bibliographies; other aspects of this order have been passed down orally and have today become legendary.

Who were these knights, and what is it about the Knights Templar that has made their legacy survive the centuries? Why do they continue to be the most recognized order of knights over other knightly orders of the Crusades? These men weren't simply monks, soldiers, or warriors; they were men of their times, so their attitudes and actions cannot possibly be equated to those of modern man.

To know everything there is to know about this order of knights would require the reading of dozens, if not hundreds, of books, manuscripts, and documents. However, even a brief glimpse into their history is a fascinating journey into the past and into a different age, one that was surrounded and consumed by cultural and political battles and wars, not merely for the sake of land or kingdoms but also for personal salvation.

Discovering the truth about this order is challenging for historians, as the Templars' central archive in Cyprus was destroyed in 1571 by the Turks. However, records of the order have been found in libraries, private collections, and archives that contain information about the more mundane aspects of accounting, such as sheep farming. Some of these records have not yet been translated or further examined by historians or scholars, perhaps because they are scattered in countries throughout Europe.

The Knights Templar Stand Out

It can be said that the Knights Templar could be equated to the special forces today, elite military units that exist in many countries around the world. These knights were a different breed since they were expected to be trained in a different fashion than the "usual" knights of the realm.

Based on a letter written by Abbot Bernard of Clairvaux and received by the founder of the Knights Templar, Hugh de Payns, the Knights Templar were to be held to a higher standard than other orders of knights, especially the Knights Hospitaller, the undisputed rivals of the Knights Templar.

The abbot instructed that the Knights Templar should not only fight against heretics, heathens, and pagans but also drive back the invisible evils that plagued men's souls.

While the Knights Templar were not monks as we think of monks today, they were a dedicated and holy military unit that fought for

Christianity. They were willing to forgo the temptations of the flesh and comforts of life to better serve God and their order.

While the Templars were not true monks, they are today often referred to as warrior monks. They were required to take vows of obedience, chastity, and poverty, similar to other knightly orders, but they were also formed to specifically provide military defense rather than the other way around. At the time, the concept of a knight was not one only engaged in a physical battle against the enemies of the church but also one who held a depth of spiritual devotion that might seem impossible to achieve. Over time, the Templars proved themselves capable of doing that very thing, and thus, the concept of a warrior monk was born.

In the medieval ages, the concept of knighthood was not a singular concept, such as the perceived ideals of the Knights of the Round Table of lore, nor even of secular knights who belonged to knightly fraternities. The Knights Templar was a new idea of knighthood, one that was born, specifically by Abbot Bernard, to turn knights away from behaviors that he considered unsavory, undignified, and unworthy. Such behaviors included playing games, storytelling, jousting, and gambling. He was displeased with the pride that many knights of the day displayed with their way of dress or the way they coveted material things. He believed that knights should set a higher example and live up to them.

Not all knights in the Knights Templar or in other orders were considered full knights. Only full Templar knights, known as knight-brothers, were given permission to wear the recognizable white mantle with the red cross emblazoned upon it. In many cases, full knights were limited to those who came from the upper echelons of society, but at the beginning of the order, knight-brothers were more of a separate society or caste to maintain this distinction.

Many knight-brothers already had the monetary wherewithal to pay for their horses, equipment, and clothing, such as their mantle or religious habit, which, depending on rank, was either white or black. During the early years of the order, they wore no mantle, instead opting to wear ordinary and simple clothes. Many of them were already trained in knightly skills, and after they were accepted into the Templars as a full knight-brother, they received additional weapons.

What about the lower echelons of the Knights Templar, those who were not considered full knights? Sergeants or lesser positions of authority were allowed to wear black tunics with the red cross emblazoned on the front and back of their mantles, which were either black or brown, contrary to the knight-brothers of the order, who were allowed to wear the white mantle with the red cross.

The Pilgrims and the Templars

Over the centuries, especially as pilgrims ventured to the Holy Land in the early 14th century, it became increasingly vital that they be protected. The pilgrimages of later crusade years became larger and included not only those among the "common masses" but also nobles, business owners, and others considered of higher status.

Pilgrimages before and shortly after the First Crusade had been spurred by the pilgrims themselves, who sought to make the journey as a penance of sacrifice and hoped for the forgiveness of a variety of sins. By the early 14th century, the journey was often considered *expected* of individuals by the church. One might even say required. Even so, like the centuries before, the journey was difficult and challenging.

During the early 14th century, the Knights Templar owned many ships and often granted hundreds of pilgrims passage on them for a great part of their journey to the Holy Land. Traveling by sea cut off many months of arduous travel by land. Even so, it could still take nearly a year for pilgrims from England to reach Italy before they stepped upon the shores of the Holy Land. Travel by boat over the Mediterranean Sea could take anywhere from four to six weeks, depending on weather and tides. So, they traveled by land and by sea to unknown destinations, crossing strange territories in the process. Pirates also preyed on pilgrims, but pirates likely stayed away from Templar ships when their banners or insignia were emblazoned on their sails. Still, it was a journey filled with uncertainty and fear. Many were never heard from again.

Pilgrimages to the Holy Land were strongly encouraged by the church. And pilgrims were not just men; women and even children were encouraged to travel to see the holy sites as well. To those at the time, a pilgrimage was seen as a badge of faith or a journey of the pious.

Of course, there were also those who were less pious among these groups, many of them criminals who were told to take the journey to atone for their crimes and sins. These criminal pilgrims or penitents had to take an oath before local authorities before they left, promising to purge their hearts and minds of evil thoughts and deeds. Only then were they given something known as a safe conduct document that displayed the crime for which they had been charged. The criminals had to show these documents and get them stamped or marked by a variety of religious authorities whenever they were asked for them. When they approached any holy city, shrines, churches, or religious landmarks, they had to show the religious authorities these documents before they were allowed to visit.

Also among the pilgrims were those who had been charged with heresy. To tell everyone apart, criminals were told to wear a chain somewhere on their body, sometimes around their neck or their waist. Heretics might be told to wear a black garment with a white cross emblazoned on the front and the back.

During the 13th century, pilgrimages had grown so large and were nearly constant that French authorities forbade pilgrimages to Rome for a while, fearing that their own population would decrease.

However, most of those individuals seeking to make a pilgrimage did so to pay their respects to the Christian saints and relics, particularly at sites found within the city of Jerusalem, the holiest of cities.

Note of interest: Badges

It became relatively common during the Crusades for "badges" to be created to demark a particular landmark, shrine, or destination, much like stickers can be found on cars or suitcases today to denote places a person visited.

In the days of the pilgrimages, these badges were unique to a specific location or shrine. Some pilgrims collected them as mementos or to verify that they had truly been to Rome, Jerusalem, or other important sites. For some, these badges became a symbol of their dedication.

For others, these badges were used as bragging rights. And like modern times, these badges were often falsely manufactured, traded, bartered for, and so forth. This was frowned upon. The Knights Templar knew of the practice, but they never designed or manufactured any badges for their assistance or transportation of pilgrims.

Templar Fortifications

Throughout Europe and the Middle East, churches and castles were erected by the Templars, many of which had been given to the knights with the purpose of protecting routes to Jerusalem and other holy cities. Over time, the Knights Templar were charged with the safety and protection of great spans of land, and they built garrisons and castles in places called Aragon, Chastel Blanc, and Ponferrada.

Some locations are more well known, such as the Templar holdings in Jerusalem (their quarters under Solomon's Temple) on the Temple Mount, believed to be the original site of the temple built by King Solomon. There was another Templar stronghold at Acre, where the knights fought the Saracens before staging a retreat to the island of Cyprus.

Pilgrim Castle today.

Remnants of the castle known as Château Pèlerin, also known as Atlit or Pilgrim Castle, can be seen today in Haifa, a port city in Israel. This castle had only stood for just over seventy years prior to its abandonment by the Knights Templar following the loss of Acre to the Turks in 1291. It was a strong fortress that boasted it could hold four thousand knights

The ancient keep of Chastel Blanc in modern-day Safita, Syria, towers over a spit of land jutting into the Mediterranean Sea. The castle was destroyed in 1171, but one can still see remains of the keep today. The keep had officers' quarters, a garrison, and a chapel. It also boasted a warning bell tower that sounded an alarm upon sight of any suspected hostiles.

Art of the ruins of Ruad Fortress.

An island fortress on Ruad Island in Syria is known to be the last stronghold of the Templars in the Middle East. It boasted infantry, knights, and archers. The story associated with this stronghold is a sad one. After a siege by the Muslims, a surrender was negotiated. The knights of the garrison were promised safe passage, but following the ceasefire, the negotiations were rendered null and void when the Muslims broke their word and executed the infantry and the archers. They banished the remnants of the Templar garrison to a prison in Cairo.

A keep on the island of Cyprus became the headquarters of the Knights Templar in the Holy Land. Other castles of the Knights Templar could be found in what is today Hungary, Croatia, Italy, Poland, and Switzerland.

Churches of the Templars sprouted out just about everywhere they trod, and their inspiration in design and structure mimicked the Church of the Holy Sepulchre in Jerusalem, especially the rounded sides that were popular throughout Europe at the time. One of these churches is known as the Church of the Holy Sepulchre, also known as the Round Church, which was built in Cambridge, England, around 1130. The London headquarters of the Templars in central London and the Temple Church still stand today.

The Templars' architectural acumen and skills are well displayed around the world, from round churches to those with a dozen sides (for example, the Safed castle built between 1240 and 1244, as well as Pilgrim Castle, which was built in 1218). Of course, other knightly orders, such as the Knights Hospitaller, also built churches and chapels in the round form.

The Rules of Templar Life

The Knights Templar gained a reputation fighting not only for Christianity and all it encompasses but also for their own order. Historically, the Knights Templar was a highly disciplined unit, but at the same time, the men often forgot about their own sense of unity for the sake of personal glory or vengeance. These knights were known for being incredibly brave, but they were still men who could be ruled by their emotions, making them reckless.

One of the most important documents that still exist about the Templars emphasizes what was expected of a Templar knight. This document is known as the Rule of the Templars. The Rule was not only a guideline of expectations regarding behavior; more importantly, it instilled a sense of obedience in the knights. As a code of conduct, it covered a variety of topics, including how they were to eat their meals, what their clothing was to look like, and a number of other restrictions regarding socializing and even sleeping arrangements.

Originally, the Rule included sixty-eight directives, but eventually, because of the growth of the Knights Templar, it ended up including several hundred. Punishment for not obeying the rules varied. Some of these rules were common sense, while others, at least by today's standards, were extreme and maybe even amusing.

It's impossible to list all of the rules here, but we will paraphrase some so you can get an idea of the Templars' standards.

The Knights Templar were allowed to eat meat only three times a week except under certain circumstances, such as All Saints' Day,

Christmas Day, the day honoring the Feast of the Apostles, and the Day of Assumption. Back then, the common consensus among the order was that eating flesh (meat) had the potential to corrupt the physical body.

The habits or robes worn by the Knights Templar were to be of one solid color, either black, brown, or white. They were encouraged to wear white robes and cloaks to symbolize a life lived in purity. The color white also signified a bond with the lighter aspects of life rather than darkness to further strengthen their relationship with God.

Clothing and battle gear were to be as plain as possible since this was a sign of a humble life. Personal pride in fashion or battle adornments, for men or their horses, were discouraged. The knights were not allowed to wear pointed shoes or shoes that required shoelaces, as those were things that were perceived to be worn by pagans.

Head coverings were not encouraged, and even coifs were required to be worn over a cloth cap.

Horse trappings were to be as plain and humble as possible, and no Templars could adorn his horse's tack with fancy things like silver or gold. If there were any such adornments, they had to be tarnished so that neither the owner nor others who saw them could take any pride in or covet them.

Instructions in regard to women were also covered in the Rule.

Women were portrayed as dangerous. They were considered to be temptations that might lead a knight astray. Their attendance was to be discouraged in any Templar house to ensure the knights' vows of chastity.

The knights were strongly encouraged to avoid kissing any woman, whether it was a female relative or not. They were also encouraged to resist a woman's embrace, claiming that embracing her could, in some way, encourage them to turn away from the rules of the brotherhood. By avoiding any kissing, the knights could be assured that their hearts were dedicated and devoted to God, allowing them to maintain a clean conscience.

If any Templar was found to be with a woman in a "wicked" place or with a woman of ill repute, he was to be put in irons and lose his habit or robe. He could no longer participate in elections, especially the election of the grand master, and they were not even allowed to carry their banner.

When it came to women, the Templars were cautioned about talking with women about any carnal knowledge. If one of the men was on the recipient end of such a conversation, he was supposed to immediately fall silent, and if that didn't work, he was to walk away.

It should be noted that the primary focus of such guidelines was to encourage the knights to dedicate themselves wholly and completely to the order and brotherhood and in their dedication to God and Jesus Christ. However, the foundation of the Rule, as mentioned, was to instill strict and unquestioning obedience.

Among the Rule is also a number of directives that seem petty by today's standards and probably even to many of the knights of the brotherhood back then. However, their vows of obedience required them to follow the guidelines set before them. These rules could get quite extreme. We have included a few below as examples.

Asking permission was essential in the hierarchy of the Knights Templar. No brother was allowed to do just about anything without asking permission first. That included bathing, riding their horse, taking medicine, or venturing into town.

The brothers were not allowed to make even the smallest of changes to their horse tack, which means they couldn't change their saddles, stirrups, or bridles, without getting permission first. This also applied to their own weapons as well. That meant the brother couldn't adjust the belt bearing his sword (although he could adjust the buckle) or even shorten stirrup straps without asking first. He also had to ask permission to make repairs to his helmet, his armor, or his sword.

The grand master, the headmaster of the order, was allowed to gift one man's horse, armor, or whatever else he wanted to another brother or knight, and the knight whose items were taken was not allowed to get angry or frustrated. Doing so was considered by the grand masters to go against God's will.

No brothers were allowed to receive letters from relatives or anyone else without the permission of their commander or master. Even if they had permission, and if the commander required it, the letters had to be read to him.

It may be shocking to modern readers that the Knights Templar and other orders were required to obey such extreme rules, but the need to maintain discipline and obedience should not be underestimated. These rules were meant to encourage the right frame of mind and attitude, allowing Knights Templar to be obedient on and off the battlefield. It is easy to imagine that many were frustrated by these harsh rules, but the Templars dared not show it.

In a way, the Rule was meant to encourage the knights and brothers to avoid "normal" aspects of society, allowing them to adhere to a higher standard than the average person. The Rule also encouraged the Templers to live and die by their vows and to take their positions very seriously. These rules also included aspects of wealth.

A Templar was not allowed to keep or even carry money without the permission of his master, and if one borrowed money from another, he was required to buy only what he said he needed the money for and nothing else.

In cases where a brother or knight died and was found with money on his person, in a hidden pouch or otherwise, he was to be considered a thief. Such individuals were not allowed to be buried in hallowed ground, and prayers were not to be said over them.

Even guidelines about sleeping are found in the Rule.

Brothers were required to always have a candle or other light burning throughout the night so they would not become prey to wickedness as they dreamed.

Knights and brothers were encouraged to cover up at bedtime and to sleep in their stockings, shirts, and breeches. Shirts were to be belted.

The Rule also talked about how a knight should act in battle or during times of war.

It was forbidden for any knight to attack without the commander's permission. If a knight did so, and someone was harmed because of it, he could lose his habit. However, the rules differed slightly when it came to seeing a fellow Christian in peril. If a knight believed he could help that man, then he could do so.

However, if a fellow knight behaved in a reckless or foolish manner and an enemy attacked him with the intent to kill him, a knight could leave his squad to help that man without asking permission. Once he returned to his squad, he was not to boast about it.

There were rules about traveling. The Templars journeyed far on their crusades, but they were required to respect traveling and camp rules.

The Templars were not to stray from camp any farther than they could hear the ring of a bell without permission. They were not allowed to carry any additional belongings or bags on their horses without permission either.

The Templars were not typically able to hunt for food during their journeys except for fishing. They could forage for vegetables in fields. They could take a wild animal *only* if they knew how to do so without actually hunting it.

When it came to sharing food, a brother or knight was allowed to share his food with others but only with those close enough that he could reach them with an outstretched arm. The knight with the most food was always encouraged to invite the man closest to him to share if that man so desired.

In general, the Templars were required to present a certain character that exemplified their dignity and obedience. They were required to set examples for others and not do anything that spoke of less-than-stellar behavior at any time. In this way, they were perceived as not only honest but also humble in their devotion and dedication to their faith.

During certain eras, the knights were allowed to have up to three horses and a single squire. The rules also applied to the servants and squires. The knights were also not allowed to seriously injure any slaves without permission. (Some aspects of Templar business, like many societies throughout the Middle Ages, relied on the labor provided by captives, primarily from the steppes of Russia, taken by the Turks and Mongols.) They were allowed to beat them with leather straps if it was felt they deserved it, but care had to be taken not to maim them.

Gambling without permission was allowed as long as wagers were limited to candle pieces or a crossbow. The knights were not allowed to wager horses, weapons, or anything that cost themselves or anyone else any money.

Punishments for crimes were often severe. Here are a few examples:

Any knight or brother who failed to adhere to the house commandments could have his habits or robes taken away from him, and he risked being put in irons.

If any two knights or brothers exchanged blows, he risked losing his habit or robe, and if serious injury occurred, he could be put in irons.

Any knight or brother who struck another Christian, be it a woman or a man, with a staff, stone, or otherwise sharp weapon, especially if they intended the blow to maim or kill, could lose his habit or robe.

Any brother who left without permission (absent without leave, or AWOL in today's parlance) risked losing his habit or robe for one year and one day. If he happened to keep anything in his belongings that was forbidden for more than two nights, he ran the risk of being expelled from the house.

Conflicts with the Ideals of Knighthood

Idyllic knighthood has always represented the image of chivalry, devotion to one's faith, and a never-ending duty and obligation to defend and protect the weak. These guidelines and ideals were encouraged in a number of knightly orders, especially those of the monk warriors, including the Knights Templar.

One of the requirements of the Knights Templar was to take a vow of chastity and poverty, following the example of King Arthur's knight, Sir Galahad. This rule was approved in 1128 and recommended by the co-founder of the order, Hugh de Payns. A Templar would be frowned upon if they did not perform the duties expected of them by God and their society, such as defending the church, the poor, widows, and orphans.

However, the concept of chivalry didn't always equate to the realities of war, especially on the battlefield. In many cases, battles were fought to the death, especially when fighting against non-believers, such as pagans and infidels in the Holy Land or the Baltic region.

Many castle or fortification sieges of the time were conducted in a "gentlemanly" way. In many instances, military commanders allowed surrender up until the point where the opposing forces actually scaled the walls. They would often initiate a ceasefire to allow civilians or others who had sought refuge to exit without harm. Some of these people were even given money, food, and clothing by the attacking army.

However, when defenders of these keeps, fortresses, and castles refused such clemency and insisted on carrying on with the fighting, the invading armies could effectively collect whatever riches they could find inside the walls, except for places like churches or convents.

This type of behavior didn't always happen. In some cases, the knights grew uncontrollable, which is not necessarily surprising since many lived outside of the boundaries of the law. Some had agreed to fight in exchange for pardons. The concept of chivalry was not as important to "lower-class" knights as they were to noble knights, although there were surely times when even a noble knight succumbed to temptation.

As such, many knights did not follow the code of chivalry in battles, and during moments when emotion, fear, and bloodlust filled their hearts and minds, self-discipline eroded completely in those who sought personal glory.

Even so, the brotherhoods of knights, regardless of the order, required discipline, and this was especially true of the Knights Templar, one of the most memorable orders in modern history. For over seven centuries, the reputation and the deeds of the Knights Templar have been wreathed in historical truth, legend, and rumor. So, let's take a look at how it all began.

The Origins of the Knights Templar

The origins of the Knights Templar are generally perceived by historians to have been in the modern-day Champagne region of France, known as Troyes during its time. The order came about due to the desperate need for protection of large groups of Christian pilgrims to the Holy Land around the year 1119, following the First Crusade.

A 19ᵗʰ-century painting of Hugh de Payns.
https://commons.wikimedia.org/wiki/File:Hugues_de_Payens_(Versailles).jpg

History states that the Knights Templar was developed by two men: Hugh de Payns and a man by the name of Godfrey de Saint-Omer. It is said that these two men led a mere seven men to Jerusalem, where they took vows of obedience, poverty, and chastity.

Originally, this small group was known as the Poor Fellow-Soldiers of Christ and the Temple of Solomon, though today, they are known simply as the Knights Templar. The original nine knights, known as knight-brothers, came from noble families. In the early years of the organization, they received support and aid from the ruler of Jerusalem at the time, King Baldwin II, and the patriarch of Jerusalem, Warmund of Picquigny.

At the time, the small group of Templars became associated with the Hospitallers, which had been officially recognized by the church in 1113, although the Hospitallers didn't become known as a military religious organization until the late 1130s.

King Baldwin II accommodated the small group of Templars, allowing them to stay on a portion of his palace grounds known as the Lord's Temple, what today is called the Dome of the Rock. This was the site of Solomon's Temple.

The handful of Templars soon grew in number. Within a decade, it is believed the order increased quite dramatically. Historical documents state that in the 1170s, the group had grown to three hundred knights in Jerusalem alone. The dearth of historical materials doesn't give modern historians or readers much information about what the Templars did in Jerusalem during that time other than guarding the pilgrims venturing to the city, so the first decade of their presence in Jerusalem is sketchy.

However, by 1170, some historical documents show that the order was well organized and that the Knights Templar, as well as the Hospitallers and the Knights of the Holy Sepulchre, performed similar duties in regard to providing protection and aid to pilgrims.

The Grand Masters

Knightly orders were led by a grand master, and the same was true for the Knights Templar. The office of grand master was a powerful position and not only among the knights. The grand masters often influenced other aspects of society, including politics and religion.

A grand master was expected to fulfill the position for life. As such, he would be treated with the utmost respect by religious and secular leaders. During the time of the Crusades, the grand master was given the great distinction and honor of being able to have four horses and an entourage that included but was not necessarily limited to a chaplain, two personal knights, a sergeant, a clerk, a servant (to carry his lance and shield), and a cook.

Despite the power of the grand master position, he could not declare war, wage war, or negotiate in any way without first meeting with other high-ranking officials of the order. He also faced other limitations, especially regarding funds. However, the Templar grand masters were expected to lead by example, to personify the spiritual example of a devoted life, and to lead their men into battle.

By the middle of the 1100s, grand masters had accumulated great prestige and power. When Jacques de Molay achieved the rank of grand master in the late 13th century, he oversaw nearly one thousand Templar houses, outposts, and castles throughout western Europe and the Middle East. At that time, membership likely hovered around seven thousand individuals, not counting families or those who provided ancillary services. At its peak, there were twenty thousand members.

The Templar's First Grand Master

Hugh de Payns (often spelled Hugues de Payens) was the first grand master of the Knights Templar, although a number of historians and others believe he was in the Holy Land prior to the founding of the order during the years between 1104 and 1108. In his late teens, he accompanied his half-brother, Stephen de Blois, to the region.

During the early years following the First Crusade, the Christian presence in the Middle East was still limited. They were also effectively surrounded by the Muslims, mainly the Turks. Though the First Crusade had been won by the Christians, a trek to the Holy Land was still very dangerous for pilgrims, who were more often than not under constant threat by the Turks, who still inhabited much of the region. Between the port of Jaffa and overland to Jerusalem (a distance of just over thirty miles or fifty-four kilometers), pilgrims were often accosted, robbed, and sometimes killed.

While not much is known about the Frenchman Hugh de Payns, what is known is that he was a vassal of the Champagne region and might have been part of a group that visited Jerusalem in about 1104. In the Middle Ages, specifically in feudal societies that existed at the time, a vassal was someone who oversaw a fife given to them for services rendered to a lord or nobleman. Not all vassals received fifes or properties, as some lived as household knights within their lord's court.

A vassal was also expected to side with his overlord during times of strife. At a moment's notice, the lord could demand the services of the knight for any military or other purpose. In other words, the vassal not only promised but also owed loyalty to his lord, so his refusal to serve his lord was considered a felony. It was a breach of duty and something so offensive that they would be punished severely.

In some cases, fifes were passed down through generations, from eldest son to eldest son, although circumstances often changed. For example, upon the death of a vassal, his fife could be returned to the lord or nobleman who had given it to him.

Hugh de Payns was a vassal, and although he was believed to have taken part in some actions during the First Crusade, it is not known for sure. However, he was very much involved in the origins of the Knights Templar, as was Godfrey of Saint-Omer, Archambaud of St. Agnan, and André of Montbard (uncle of Bernard of Clairvaux). They pledged to provide protection to the Christian visitors coming to Jerusalem.

Over the years, Hugh de Payns spent much time encouraging and recruiting additional knights to join the order, and he was relatively successful in this endeavor, especially once King Baldwin II of Jerusalem became determined to set his sights on Damascus. Eventually, the Templars' reputation garnered attention from Europe's powerful clergy, politicians, and citizenry.

Historical accounts mention that within a decade of their founding, the order held properties throughout Europe, and its rise to power was nearly astronomical. As it is today, the more powerful one is, the greater the wealth generated, and as can be expected, new men who joined the ranks hoped to enjoy some of that power.

The Knights Templar reached its largest membership in the 12th century, but the Templars weren't just warriors. Many of them were advisors to kings, adept at banking and financial matters, and known for guarding valuable treasuries. They were exceptionally gifted as seafarers, traders, and business owners. They became known as experts in various fields of agriculture, trade, and commerce and eventually garnered a reputation of being one of the most powerful and wealthy organizations in Europe and beyond for their time.

Of all the knightly orders of the Middle Ages, the Knights Templar, perhaps due to their extraordinary financial acumen, continue to stand out, and their name continues to be recognized well into the 21st century.

Bernard of Clairvaux

Another person heavily involved in the origins of the Knights Templar was an abbot by the name of Bernard of Clairvaux. A number of legends are connected to him, especially in his somewhat eccentric views of the Christian religion. There are stories of him diving into freezing water to squelch his "carnal" instincts as a young man. Yet at the same time, he was recognized as someone who managed to connect with his audiences as he preached, so much so that his name traveled throughout Europe, especially in France.

It is commonly believed that upon his second return from the Holy Land, he became a co-founder of the Knights Templar and heavily influenced the reorganization of the Benedictine Order (also known as the Bernardines) and the creation of a new monastery. The piece of land was known as the Valley of Light (in French *Clairvaux*), which attracted people from throughout Europe.

Organization of the Knights Templar

The organization of the Templars was structured after the typical hierarchy of other military orders of the medieval age. The grand master was at the head of it all and typically resided in the headquarters of the Knights Templar in the Holy Land. Numerous officers under the grand master were chosen to oversee vastly large territories that were eventually divided into smaller areas or provinces. Each of these, in turn, was overseen by area commanders, who themselves oversaw masters, who were responsible for overseeing individual Templar houses in a given area.

Dozens of Templar houses were founded throughout various regions, primarily to establish their presence in a territory. The houses were equipped with adequate troops and manpower, equipment, and, of course, sources of money for those fighting in the Holy Land or farther east.

Some of the primary offices of the order included the following:

Grand Master – the leading authority who answered to no one but the pope

Seneschal – the grand master's advisor or co-pilot of sorts

Marshal – in charge of anything pertaining to battle or war

Draper – in charge of dispensing knight's clothing and in charge of making sure the knights were clothed in a manner that befitted the order. As such, the draper was considered to be above all the brothers in regard to status.

Of course, there were other commanders of the Templars who had responsibilities and specifically assigned regions, such as Antioch, Jerusalem, or Tripoli.

The *infirmarer* was in charge of hospitals or infirmaries, primarily providing care to elderly brothers. During the Middle Ages, most medical services, care for the poor and the infirm, and so forth fell to the Hospitallers and other similar orders. For this reason, the Templars were primarily known as warriors who were renowned for their fighting skills.

The grand masters of the Knights Templar made their headquarters in Jerusalem from the time of their founding in about 1119 until about 1190, following the fall of Jerusalem. They then made their headquarters at Acre in around 1191 through its fall in 1291. After that, they established their headquarters in Cyprus.

Other than the founder Hugh de Payns, one name truly stands out in regard to Templar grand masters, and that is Jacques de Molay, the grand master from 1293 to 1312.

Grand Master Jacques de Molay: The Beginning of the End

The twenty-third and last grand master of the Knights Templar was the leader from 1292 until the French king, Philip IV, decimated their ranks and dissolved the order in 1312. Jacques de Molay died in 1314 after he was burned at the stake. The demise of the Knights Templar is surrounded by lies, suspicions, torture, and bravery. As such, Jacques de Molay is one of the more well-known grand masters of the order.

Image of Jacques de Molay.
https://commons.wikimedia.org/wiki/File;JacquesdeMolay.jpg

Jacques de Molay was in his twenties when he joined the Knights Templar around 1265. He fought in several battles, earning himself a good reputation as an effective leader. His reputation followed him even after the defeat of the Christian forces in Acre in 1291, and it is said that even after that loss, he made huge efforts to recapture the city.

However, there is little known about his life over the next fifteen years prior to the flurry of arrests of the Templars in France in 1307. From then until 1312, hundreds of Templars were imprisoned, tortured, and forced to confess to all sorts of claims of heresy, anti-religious behavior, and other depraved acts.

Even Jacques de Molay, who was nearing seventy years of age by this time, confessed to a number of crimes against Christianity after he was forced to endure extreme torture. However, he and others recanted, publicly claiming coercion. And when he was sentenced to death in Paris, by burning at the stake no less, he loudly recanted, claiming that the knights and his order were innocent of the claims against them and that their honor and purity were beyond question.

But how did all of this come about?

By the autumn of 1307, the Templars' reputation had gone from heroes to scapegoats, perhaps some of it being generated by jealousy or a desire for power. A number of claims against them were believed to have been brought by King Philip IV of France. In the autumn of 1307, he presented his officers across France with sealed orders with the directive not to open the orders until the evening of October 12th. The reason for his orders and demands for secrecy? These orders stated his intention to arrest every Templar in the country.

But why would he do that? Basically, it boils down to greed.

King Philip believed that he should be the one benefiting from the wealth and power accrued by the Knights Templar, but there are some rumors that he believed the Templars owed him money. However, there are also rumors that it was King Philip who owed the Templars money and that he was angry that they refused to approve additional loans to him.

King Philip didn't care for the pope at the time, Pope Boniface VIII. History relates that some of King Philip's men had been ordered to kidnap and hold the pope hostage. Pope Boniface died a short time later, and a new pope, Clement V, took his seat. Clement V was perhaps intimidated by Philip and was more than willing to partake in Philip's efforts to destroy the Knights Templar.

Before Pope Boniface VIII's demise in 1303, he was believed to have greatly admired the Knights Templar. Once Pope Boniface died, the Templars realized how much they were in danger. The first arrest came early in the morning of October 13th (a Friday), and what followed was a vicious and bloody episode in the history of the Catholic Church.

Note of interest: Friday the 13th

Friday the 13th is often considered a day of bad luck. As mentioned, the first arrests of the Knights Templar occurred on the morning of Friday, October 13th, which certainly was a day of bad luck for the Templars. Some still equate the origin of modern-day beliefs of bad luck on Friday the 13th as being founded by the blitz attack on the Knights Templar on that blackest of days.

However, the concept of the number thirteen as being negative has existed for millennia, and many point to the fact that the Templars

---

were not the only ones to face especially bad luck on Friday the 13th. It is widely believed that Christ was also crucified on a Friday, with some saying that the date possibly could have been the 13th. Although we don't know for sure what day Christ died, recent investigations claim that he died on Friday the 3rd.

The belief in unlucky number thirteen has persisted for centuries, and while the true origins of the concept of Friday the 13th is a mystery, the day is still considered to be filled with bad luck. Even today, many avoid stepping under ladders, breaking a mirror, or stepping on a crack. On Friday the 13th, people still might find it beneficial to throw salt over one's shoulder, not to cross paths with a black cat, and to keep one's home well-lit to reduce hiding places for bad spirits.

Whether King Philip chose that day to launch his attack against the Knights Templar because of the connotations with it will never be known, but the day remains one of infamy in the annals of history.

The Knights Templar were not the only targets of King Philip, as he also targeted French Jews and rich Italian merchants. At the time, Philip was filled with greed, seeking to increase his coffers. He targeted thousands of Templars who happened to reside in France at that time, including Grand Master Jacques de Molay, who had been summoned to the country from Cyprus by Pope Clement V around 1307 to discuss a potential new crusade.

Although the Knights Templar had taken vows of poverty, the order amassed great wealth through lands and their business dealings. By around 1300, few of the Templar Order were actually true knights. Many of their members were bankers or involved in finance. Historical documents state that noblemen, kings, and wealthy merchants left their riches with the Knights Templar for safekeeping. After all, no one would willingly mess with the Knights Templar.

So, how did the reputation of the Knights Templar decline so quickly? It was mostly due to rumors, much of it instigated by Philip and with the reluctant compliance of Pope Clement. In the early days of Philip's strategy against the knights, the Knights Templar was still revered and respected. The knights were feared for their might and prowess as soldiers and warriors.

Upon his arrival in France with sixty knights in the early months of 1307, Jacques spent several months engaging in discussions with the pope. Meanwhile, King Philip's men began to spread nasty rumors about the Knights Templar.

Rumors have a way of quickly becoming truths and overcoming doubt and disbelief. King Philip's spies also made attempts to insinuate themselves into the Knights Templar. Apparently, these spies created numerous charges against the Knights Templar. They not only made some of it up but also used complaints or disgruntled murmurs from former members of the order. Some people whispered that the Knights Templar engaged in black magic and horrible rituals regarding sex. Whether any of the rumors King Philip started were true or not remains a mystery, but due to the king's hatred of the Knights Templar, it can be supposed that most of them were false.

And once the people were disgruntled enough, the king pounced and sent out his orders of arrest against the Knights Templar. Unfortunately, any Templar arrested was not only to be imprisoned but also questioned. If the knight refused to tell the truth (which was really the "truth" Philip wanted to hear), he would be tortured until he did or died. This persecution was extreme, and it is believed that one of the truths that King Philip wanted to hear and obtain a confession regarded the rumor that the Knights Templar secretly renounced their belief in Christ. It was even said that they spat on the cross.

The Templars were imprisoned, isolated, and put on a diet of bread and water, all the while enduring torture. Some of the torture was quite extreme, including one method of tying a man's hands behind his back and then suspending and lifting him into the air by a rope slung over a beam with the intention of dislocating the shoulder joints. Men were tortured on the rack, a torture device also intended to dislocate joints, and some were tortured by having their feet coated with oil and then held over a fire.

Unfortunately, these torture techniques resulted in many of the Templars confessing to false charges, some sooner than others. Among those who confessed to the false charges was the grand master himself, the elderly Jacques de Molay.

Unfortunately, it wasn't just the knights who were arrested and condemned. Farmers, bankers, and other support staff were also targeted. These men were accused of a number of offenses that included but were not limited to devil worship, spitting on the cross, homosexuality, fraud, heresy, and financial corruption.

It is believed that Pope Clement V had no idea that things would go so far and was terribly shocked. Yet, at the same time, he was afraid of retribution from the Templars who had not yet been captured. However, the so-called "confessions" of the knights required him to respond to their heresy. As such, it can be said that Pope Clement V was caught between a rock and a hard place.

Ultimately, he gave papal orders to kings throughout western Europe to arrest any Templars living on their properties. While many outside of France refused to do so, the fall of the Knights Templar had effectively begun when a vast number of them were arrested in France.

The trials and hearings of these unfortunate knights took place between 1307 and 1314, the year Grand Master Jacques de Molay died. Some historical documents state that while King Philip and Pope Clement V had discussed the possible arrests of Templars in France, the pope claimed that he had not been informed about the arrests going forward, hence the questions about whether the pope had actually approved of King Philip's actions.

Because King Philip required Pope Clement's "approval" for the hunting down, capture, torture, and even death of the Templars for legitimacy, he placed pressure on the pope until he finally agreed to allow the king to proceed. Still, the pope "interfered" by insisting that all proper procedures be followed, delaying the process for years.

It is perhaps not surprising that many of the Templars who confessed to these salacious claims later recanted their confessions, including Jacques de Molay, since those confessions had been given under torture. As a result, additional trials and hearings were conducted, which dragged on for some time. However, most of these prisoners were kept in dungeons and jail cells for years before King Philip, perhaps as a last slap in the face, had roughly fifty of them burned at the stake in 1310, with Pope Clement V apparently looking the other way, perhaps fearful of King Philip's wrath being directed at him next.

In 1311, the pope met with cardinals and King Philip at the Council of Vienne. While the Order of the Knights Templar was declared not guilty of the charges that had been brought against it, the pope believed its reputation had been so badly damaged that it would no longer be able to defend Christendom. However, it was determined that the leaders of the order could still be charged guilty.

In 1312, Pope Clement officially dissolved the Order of the Knights Templar. In total, roughly 127 charges had been brought against the Knights Templar, and while none of the charges were verified, and the order was found not guilty, their leaders paid the price of King Philip's resentment and greed.

Four of the leaders of the Knights Templar, including Jacques de Molay and Geoffrey de Charney, were brought before a small group of French cardinals and religious theologians and condemned to life imprisonment. At this time, de Molay and de Charney denied any confessions they had made. Nevertheless, their fate was sealed, as they were charged as being relapsed heretics. They were turned over to King Philip, who, without consulting the pope, sentenced them to death by burning at the stake.

So, in the early months of 1314, Grand Master Jacques de Molay, an elderly man, was burned at the stake in Paris, France, along with other Templar leaders. The might of the Knights Templar faded, but the order's story has not.

The riches, lands, and money of the knights living in France were taken by King Philip. Although he kept some of the riches, most of the vast wealth of the Knights Templar was given to the Knights Hospitaller. Many remaining Templars fled France, while others joined orders, such as the Hospitallers. The rest faded into history.

Rumors and myths

Numerous rumors and myths regarding the Knights Templar exist today, including one that suggests these knights were the first to sail across the Atlantic Ocean to the New World after the initial voyages of the Vikings. The rationale for this rumor is that numerous gravestones with Templar insignia were found in Nova Scotia.

Note of interest: Roger de Flor

One Templar by the name of Roger de Flor made quite a name for himself as a naval commander in the late 13th century. He led mercenaries and mounted knights from Catalan. He gained the reputation of being a fierce and powerful commander, especially on the high seas. In fact, after he married into a Byzantine royal family, he actually held the title of Caesar, which was quite impressive in

---

those days.

In Roger's earlier years, he served as a shipmate on a Templar ship in Marseille, France. By the time he was twenty years old, he had served as a sergeant-brother in the Knights Templar and had taken part in several battles. He also took part in the evacuation of the Templars at the Battle of Acre in 1291. At the time, the young man appeared to have been tempted by some of the riches that were being evacuated from the city and took it upon himself to appropriate some of them for his own use. Unfortunately, Grand Master Jacques de Molay learned about it and not only denounced Roger but also expelled him from the order.

Ultimately, Roger de Flor fled. Because he was so gifted at sailing, he became a successful pirate in the later medieval ages. As such, a legend blossomed that the well-known black pirate flag with the skull and bones upon it, nicknamed the Jolly Roger, was named for him. Whether truth or fiction, it is a rumor that has followed the privateer over the centuries.

Over time, a number of conspiracy theories have been born regarding the Knights Templar, such as rumors of secret societies and missions. There is no doubt that a number of rumors damaged the reputation of the Knights Templar, such as the claims made against them by King Philip, which led leading to their eventual downfall.

Even today, centuries after the remaining Knights Templar went into hiding following the debacle in France, it is believed that some traveled across the oceans and seas, some to the far reaches of Europe and some as far north as Scotland. Tunnels with Templar emblems have been found under Scottish castles.

Rumors continue to endure even after the demise of the Knights Templar. One of those rumors was that they hid a number of priceless artifacts and treasures during the early months of their persecution. Some of these treasures have become myths and still encourage treasure hunters to this day. You also might hear of these treasures in popular movies and books.

Supposedly, the Knights Templar possessed the Holy Grail, the cup Jesus sipped during the Last Supper with his disciples before his crucifixion. Another religious relic the Templars supposedly hid was the Ark of the Covenant, the wooden chest that held the original Ten

Commandments, the stone tablets that had been brought down from Mount Sinai by Moses himself. Such rumors have not been substantiated yet, but many hope to be able to prove their veracity.

Historical accounts, even while the Templars retained their might, specify a number of relics revered by the knights. The Templars are believed to have carefully stored precious objects and guarded them carefully within the walls of monasteries, cathedrals, and shrines. These relics could have included a piece of the True Cross, the bones or clothing of saints, or items closely associated with the crucifixion, such as the nails or the crown of thorns.

It is believed and historically written that a number of sojourners and crusaders returning from the Holy Land brought a number of religious objects with them, so the Templars were far from the only ones to do. The Hospitallers also have a history of being in possession of such relics.

Even the Rule of the Knights Templar mentions the protection of a revered piece of the True Cross that was carried with them on their crusades and how it was to be guarded and protected. However, it is believed that the order's True Cross was ultimately captured during the Battle of Hattin in the year 1187 by the Ayyubids. One legend surrounding this event claims that a Templar knight escaped with it and buried it quickly in the sand, but when he returned to find it later, he could not remember exactly where he had buried it. Others say the Ayyubids sent it to Damascus, placing it upside down on a lance.

The order made it known that it possessed the crown of thorns, and on Holy Thursday, the priests of the order brought it out for all to see.

Unfortunately, no historical documents have provided any indisputable evidence that the Knights Templar ever possessed the Holy Grail, the Ark of the Covenant, or the Shroud of Turin, the burial shroud of Christ. However, it is believed, based on historical documents and the Rule, that they might have owned a piece of the True Cross, a piece of the crown of thorns, and even a small vial of Christ's blood. Of course, none of this is known for sure. Some historians believe these legendary artifacts were never in possession of the Templars. They believe it made a nice story after the Templars' downfall and further added to the Templars' mystique.

It is also believed that some testimony regarding ownership of these relics cannot be verified because of the torture the knights faced during the later years of the order's existence. However, King Philip II of France ordered that Templar relics, documents, and archives, along with their land and properties, should be given to the Hospitallers, though he kept some of that wealth for himself. The Templar archives were destroyed in 1571 following the Turkish attack on Cyprus. It is likely some things about the Templars will forever be shrouded in mystery.

Conclusion

The Knights Hospitaller, the Knights of the Holy Sepulchre, the Order of St. Lazarus, the Teutonic Knights, and the Knights Templar were not the only orders of knights that existed during the Middle Ages. Some are better known than others, but regardless, these military orders, which saw action in many of the Crusades, live on today. In fact, many of the orders continue to exist.

These crusaders evoke an image of bravery and valor, of dedication to a cause and the willingness to sacrifice for that cause. Some crusades and their leaders are well known and written about in history books, but there are also numerous smaller battles, wars, and crusaders that will likely never get the attention they deserve.

The legacy of these brothers-in-arm endures, as do many of their missions. Their leaders and their reputations have been passed down for generations, and the concept of chivalry is still epitomized by envisioning these knights of old.

Numerous books have been written about many of these knightly orders, some with more historical documentation to rely on than others. Still, much of their history is wreathed in an aura of mystery and intrigue. Not everything can be found in the annals of history, such as all of the disagreements between kings and popes and the seemingly never-ending disputes of men.

Whether the knights of old took upon the mantle for religious reasons or pride is debated, but there is no doubt that many felt it was their duty to serve. The legends and histories of many of these knights maintain their place in history. They lived in troubled, dark, and uncertain times, and they followed their beliefs, many of them until their bloody and violent deaths.

Here's another book by Captivating History that you might like

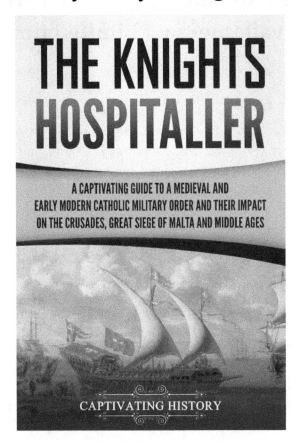

Free Bonus from Captivating History (Available for a Limited time)

Hi History Lovers!

Now you have a chance to join our exclusive history list so you can get your first history ebook for free as well as discounts and a potential to get more history books for free! Simply visit the link below to join.

Captivatinghistory.com/ebook

Also, make sure to follow us on Facebook, Twitter and Youtube by searching for Captivating History.

References

Knights Templar Encyclopedia. Ralls, Karen, Ph.D. 2007, Career Press, Franklin Lakes, NJ

The Illustrated History of Knights and Crusades. Phillips, Charles, 2010, Anness Publishing, UK

"Blessed Gerard (the Rules of Raymond du Puy)." http://blessed-gerard.org/bgt_rule.htm

"Blessed Raymond du Puy." http://www.smom-za.org/saints/raymond.htm

"The Becket Story: Archbishop Thomas Becket." https://thebecketstory.org.uk/pilgrimage/st-thomas-becket

"The Great Schism." https://education.nationalgeographic.org/resource/great-schism

"Knights of the Holy Sepulchre." https://cnewa.org/magazine/knights-of-the-holy-sepulchre-30042/

"World History Encyclopedia – Medieval Knight." https://www.worldhistory.org/Medieval_Knight/

"The First Crusade – World History.org." https://www.worldhistory.org/First_Crusade/

"History.com – The Middle Ages." https://www.history.com/topics/middle-ages/middle-ages

"The Hospitallers of St. John of Jerusalem." https://www.ewtn.com/catholicism/library/hospitallers-of-st-john-of-jerusalem-10553

"The Order of Malta." https://www.orderofmalta.int/about-the-order-of-malta/knights-of-malta/

"Catholic Answers/Encyclopedia: Knights of the Holy Sepulchre."
https://www.catholic.com/encyclopedia/knights-of-the-holy-sepulchre

"Godfrey of Bouillon." https://www.newadvent.org/cathen/06624b.htm

"World History – Visigoth." https://www.worldhistory.org/visigoth/

"PubMed – Mycobacterium leprae: A Historical study on the origins of
leprosy and its social stigma."
https://www.ncbi.nlm.nih.gov/pmc/articles/PMC8805473/#:~:text=Treatment
%20of%20leprosy%20has%20undergone,Guy%20Faget%20of%20Carville.

"Military and Hospitaller Order of Saint Lazarus of Jerusalem."
https://stlazarus.onmessagecomms.co.uk/sites/default/files/media/files/history_
key_dates_leaflet_0420_final.pdf

"Fall of Constantinople." https://www.history.com/topics/middle-
east/constantinople#fall-of-constantinople

"Knights Templar – Important Castles and Churches."
https://www.knighttemplar.org/single-post/2018/03/16/knights-templar-s-
important-castles-and-churches

"The Templars' 'curse' on the King of France."
https://blog.nationalarchives.gov.uk/templars-curse-king-france/

"April 3, AD 33: Why we believe we can know the exact date Jesus died."
https://cbs.mbts.edu/2020/04/08/april-3-ad-33-why-we-believe-we-can-know-
the-exact-date-jesus-died/

"Teutonic Knights." https://www.worldhistory.org/Teutonic_Knight/

"Teutonic Knights."
https://www.newworldencyclopedia.org/entry/Battle_of_Tannenberg_(1410)

"Teutonic Knights."
https://www.newworldencyclopedia.org/entry/Teutonic_Knights

"Frederick 'Barbarossa.'" https://www.britannica.com/place/Italy/Institutional-
reforms

"Knights Templar Rules." https://www.history.com/news/the-knights-templar-
rulebook-included-no-pointy-shoes-and-no-kissing-mom

"The Nine Worthies." https://www.ancient-origins.net/history-famous-
people/nine-worthies-are-these-most-chivalrous-men-history-007416

"Templars Being Burned at the Stake."
https://www.carmichaeldigitalprojects.org/hist447/items/show/132

Printed in the USA
CPSIA information can be obtained
at www.ICGtesting.com
LVHW021336101123
763510LV00006B/149

9 781637 168301